NE〇 ZIPANG
21ST-CENTURY JAPAN
PRESENTED BY AYUMU TAKAHASHI & EXILE ÜSA

高橋歩・EXILE ÜSA 編著

13世紀の冒険家、マルコポーロは言った。
「東に、黄金の国、ジパングがある」と。

それに影響され、
世界中の冒険家や海賊たちは、
黄金を求め、「ジパング」を目指した。

* * *

"To the east lies Zipang, the Land of Gold."
13th-century Italian explorer Marco Polo's proclamation spurred
generations of adventurers and pirates to Japan in search of their own gold.

あれから700年以上の時が流れ
21世紀の現在。

古くからの伝統と、
最先端の技術をうまくミックスしながら、
日本という国は、変わることなく、
魅力的な宝物を、生み出し続けている。

伝統 × 最新
21世紀の日本には、
素晴らしいヒト・モノ・コトが溢れている！

＊　＊　＊

Seven centuries on, 21st-century Japan continues to conceive new and alluring treasures, ingeniously blending ancient traditions and cutting-edge technology.

Tradition × Innovation
21st-century Japan abounds with wonderful people, things, and ideas.

ネオ・ジパング！

今でも日本は、黄金の国だ。

* * *

NEO ZIPANG!

Japan, still a Land of Gold.

はじめに

若い頃から、妻と、家族と、仲間と共に、世界中を放浪してきた。

そして、旅をすればするほど、感じたんだ。

「やっぱり、日本ってスゴい!」

んじゃ、なにがスゴいの?
それを伝えられる本を創りたいと想ったのが、すべてのはじまりだった。

でも、僕らは、学者や研究者ではなく、ただの旅人なので。
日本のあらゆるジャンルを網羅した「日本○○全集」でもなく、
ひとつの項目を深く掘り下げる「専門書」でもなく、
誰もが気軽に読めて、見て楽しめて、
ワクワクするお宝がいっぱい詰まった宝箱のような本を創ってみよう!

そんな想いを胸に、もう、20年のつきあいになる旅仲間、
エグザイル・ウサと一緒に、試行錯誤しながら、僕らなりの視点で、僕らなりの感性で、
21世紀ニッポンの「これ、すごくない?」を、厳選して紹介させてもらった。

さらに、日本の魅力を外国人に伝えるツールとしても、わかりやすく便利に使えるように、
ビジュアルを多めに、文章も日英のバイリンガルにした。

中高生からお年寄りまで、日本人である僕らが、
「へぇ〜、そうなんだ」「えっ、知らなかった!」「今度、ここ行ってみようか」なんて、
日本という国の楽しさを、あらためて、再発見したり。

まだ、日本を知らない外国人、もしくは、もっと日本を知りたい外国人が、
日本のことを、大好きになってくれたり。

そんなきっかけになれたら嬉しいな、と想っています。
それでは、ゆっくり、お楽しみください。

高橋歩　2019年6月　TOKYO

Prologue

I have roamed the world since my youth, with my friends, my wife, and my family.
The more I traveled, the more I came to realize that Japan is a truly amazing country.
So, what exactly is so amazing about Japan?
This question, and the search for its answer, became the catalyst for this book.

To be honest, we are neither academics nor researchers, but world travelers.
In light of this, we didn't attempt to make an exhaustive, all-inclusive guide to everything that is great about Japan, or a specialty guide to any specific area, but rather set out to assemble a trove of exciting treasures and discoveries that is easy and fun for anyone to read.

With that in mind, I linked up with travel partner and friend of 20 years EXILE ÜSA and together we embarked on a journey of trial and error to introduce a selection of amazing things in 21st-century Japan based on our own perspectives and opinions.

In order to better share the treasures of Japan with the world and enhance reading pleasure, we have incorporated a rich array of illustrations and made all the text bilingual.

Everyone from students to the elderly in Japan will find new and exciting information, little known secrets and hidden treasures within these pages; a way to re-discover the joys of their home country.

It's also a way for people in other countries to learn about Japan, and for foreigners living in Japan to find out more about this country.
Essentially, it's a way to fall in love with Japan.

We hope you will enjoy discovering a new perspective on the wonders of Japan within these pages.

Ayumu Takahashi   June, 2019 Tokyo

CONTENTS
目　次

PROLOGUE
by Ayumu Takahashi ►P2

PART 1
SPECIALITY
スペシャル
P17

日本という国のキャラクター紹介

PART 2
TREASURE
世界に誇る日本の宝物
P68

日本発祥の面白いモノを紹介

PART 3
NEO CULTURE
伝統×最新
P144

21世紀のネオカルチャーを紹介

EPILOGUE
ÜSA's Dream Note ►P212

21世紀 日本に溢れる
素晴らしい ヒト・モノ・コト
Wonderful people,things and ideasin 21st-century Japan

PART 1

SPECIALITY
スペシャル / 日本という国のキャラクター紹介
A character sketch of Japan

❶「季節の変化を楽しむ国」 ▶P20
SEASON LIFE

❷「多くの神様を持つ国」 ▶P26
EIGHT MILLION GODS

❸「4つの文字を使い分ける国」 ▶P32
FOUR ALPHABETS

❹「長寿の国」 ▶P38
LONGEVITY

❺「安心&安全な国」 ▶P44
SAFETY & PEACE

❻「戦後に驚異的な高度経済成長を遂げた国」 ▶P50
ECONOMIC GROWTH

❼「世界唯一の被爆国であり、平和憲法のある国」 ▶P56
ATOMIC BOMBING & PEACE CONSTITUTION

❽「感謝の国」 ▶P62
DAILY APPRECIATION

PART 2

TREASURE
A character sketch of Japan
世界に誇る日本の宝物 / 日本発祥の面白いモノを紹介
Precious cultural heritages and intriguing inventions from Japan

 ❶「温水洗浄便座」SPRAY TOILET SEATS ▶P70

 ❷「自動販売機」VENDING MACHINES ▶P78

 ❸「食品サンプル」REPLICA FOOD SAMPLES ▶P84

 ❹「折り紙」ORIGAMI (PAPER FOLDING) ▶P90

 ❺「寿司」SUSHI ▶P98

 ❻「温泉」ONSEN (HOT SPRING / SPA) ▶P106

 ❼「盆栽」BONSAI (THE ART OF MINIATURE TREES AND SHRUBS) ▶P114

 ❽「木造建築技術」WOODEN BUILDINGS ▶P122

 ❾「マンガ・アニメ」MANGA & ANIME ▶P130

 ❿「カプセルホテル」CAPSULE HOTELS ▶P136

PART 3

NEO CALTURE
伝統×最新 / 21世紀のネオカルチャーを紹介
Neo-culture merging tradition and technology

❶ 「日本画 × ガンダム」 ▶P146
TRADITIONAL JAPANESE PAINTINGS × GUNDAM

❷ 「花火 × 最先端テクノロジー」 ▶P156
FIREWORKS × CUTING EDGE TECHNOLOGY

❸ 「茶道 × 現代ライフスタイル」 ▶P166
TEA CEREMONY × MODERN LIFESTYLE

❹ 「歌舞伎 × 最新デジタル技術」 ▶P174
KABUKI × LATEST DIGITAL TECHNOLOGY

❺ 「和太鼓 × プロジェクションマッピング」 ▶P182
JAPANESE DRUMS × PROJECTION MAPPING

❻ 「伝統楽器 × ダンスミュージック」 ▶P190
TRADITIONAL INSTRUMENTS × DANCE MUSIC

❼ 「田んぼ × アート」 ▶P196
RICE PADDIES × ART

❽ 「竹 × 照明デザイン」 ▶P204
BAMBOO × LIGHTING DESIGN

21世紀
日本に溢れる
素晴らしい
ヒト・モノ・コト

NEO ZIPANG

21ST-CENTURY JAPAN

PRESENTED BY AYUMU TAKAHASHI & EXILE ÜSA

SPECIALITY
スペシャル

日本という国のキャラクター紹介
A character sketch of Japan

現在、世界には196の国があります。

世界全体を見渡してみたときに、
日本って、どんな国なんだろう？
他の国と比べて、どんな特徴があるんだろう？

すべての特徴をあげてもキリがないので、
ここでは、僕らの実感やリアルなデータをもとに、
「ニッポン。ここは、スペシャルでしょ！」
そんな8つの視点を紹介してみました。

まずは、日本という国のキャラクターを、
ふんわりと感じてみましょう。

There are 196 countries in the world.
When compared with the rest of the world, what kind of country is Japan,
and what sets Japan apart from other countries?
Trying to list all the unique characteristics of Japan would be futile, so we
narrowed it down to eight things we think are particularly special based on
our own sentiments and hard data.

Read on for a better understanding about the character of Japan.

日本の基本情報

【人口】 1億2,748万人（世界10位 / 世界196カ国中）※出典:World Population Prospects 2017

【面積】 37万7,972km²（世界61位 / 世界196カ国中）※出典:FAO 2015

【人口密度】 347人/km²（世界35位 / 世界196カ国中）※出典:WORLD BANK 2017

【経済規模（GDP）】 4兆8,840億ドル（世界3位 / 世界196カ国中）※出典:CIA 2017

【軍事費】 5兆3,596億円（世界8位 / 世界196カ国中）※出典:ストックホルム国際平和研究所 2017

Basic Information

【Population】 127,480,000 (10th of 196 countries)
Source: World Population Prospects 2017

【Area】 377,972km² (61st of 196 countries)
Source: FAO 2015

【Population Density】 347/km² (35th of 196 countries)
Source: WORLD BANK 2017

【GDP】 4.9 trillion dollars (3rd of 196 countries)
Source: CIA 2017

【Military Spending】 5.4 trillion yen (8th of 196 countries)
Source: Stockholm International Peace Research Institute 2017

四季 Shi Ki

SPECIALITY ①

春夏秋冬。世界中に四季がある国は、いくつかありますが、日本ほど、美しい四季を持ち、季節の移り変わりを繊細に意識しながら、多彩に楽しんでいる国は、他に例がないと思います。

季節の変化を楽しむ国

SEASONAL LIFE

Spring, summer, fall and winter.
While Japan is not the only country with four distinct seasons,
what sets Japan apart is the beauty of each season,
and nationwide appreciation for the details of each subtle change in season.

「二十四節気」

日本の季節は、春夏秋冬といった「4つの季」に加えて、さらに、立春、夏至、秋分、冬至など、「24の節」に分かれています。そして、1年中、その時季ならではの自然現象、旬の味覚、独自の習慣などが全国に無数にあり、それが、日常のニュースなどでも、普通に話題にされています。

Aside from the four seasons, Japan also recognizes 24 *sekki* (divisions) of the year such as the spring and fall equinoxes, summer and winter solstices, and other dates based on natural phenomena. Throughout the year, innumerable special events and foods are enjoyed throughout the country to celebrate many of these subtle changes in seasons and they are an intrinsic part of daily life.

古い時代から、日本人は、季節によって移り変わる自然現象に名前を付ける名人です。「風」にも「微風（そよ風）」「春一番」「木枯らし」などわずかな違いに応じて2000種類以上の名前があり、「雨」にも「鉄砲雨」「霧雨（きりさめ）」「夕立」など400種類以上、「雪」にも「粉雪」「牡丹雪」「なごり雪」など100種類を超える名前があります。

Since ancient times, people in Japan have been adept at coming up with names for natural phenomena that change with the seasons. There are over 2,000 names for the various winds that blow at different times of the year from gentle breezes to spring storms and winter winds that blow leaves from trees. The 400 names for rain include 'gun rain', 'misty rain' and 'evening shower'. Snow has over 100 names to describe everything from light powder to large flakes and snow in late spring.

日本の俳句では、季語（きご）と呼ばれる、特定の季節を表す言葉を含むのが決まりとなっています。季語は、「歳時記」と呼ばれる書物に採集されるという形で増え続けており、現代の歳時記では、5000語を超える季語が収録されています。

Conventional haiku, short Japanese poems with three lines comprised of 5, 7 and 5 'on' or syllables, must contain a 'kigo,' or seasonal reference. A collection of these seasonal references, known as 'Saijiki,' now tops 5,000 words referencing specific seasons, with more being added through time.

現在も、世界中で人気を博している、寿司、和食、盆栽、お祭り、花火などの日本独特な文化が生まれた背景には、古くから日本に受け継がれている、季節の移り変わりをカラフルに、そして、繊細に楽しめる感性が、大きく影響していると思います。

The emergence of globally popular Japanese foods and traditions such as sushi, *washoku* (Japanese cuisine), bonsai, festivals and fireworks is due in large part to the unique sense Japanese have of enjoying the details of the changing seasons with flair, a sense that has been fostered through the generations since ancient times.

日本では、古くから、
八百万（やおよろず）の神といって、
多くの神様がいます。
ひとりでもなく、複数でもなく、
ありとあらゆるところに神様がいます。

SPECIALITY ❷

多くの神様を持つ国

EIGHT MILLION GODS

In Japan, it has long been said that there are eight million gods.
Not one god, nor several, but a god in every thing in existence.

世界には、一神教、多神教、無神教など、様々な文化がありますが、日本の場合、神様の数は桁違いです。
草にも木にも、鳥にも魚にも、道具にも家にも、風にも雨にも、惑星にも素粒子にも……すべてに魂が宿り、ありとあらゆるところに神様がいます。

Some cultures around the world are monotheistic, others polytheistic, and still others atheistic. The number of gods in Japan, however, is unmatched, with a long-held belief that every blade of grass and tree, every bird and fish, every tool and house, even the wind and rain, the planets and the elementary particles have their own spirit. In Japan, gods are everywhere, in everything.

日本人の精神は、いい意味で、「いいとこどり」。
クリスマスをやって、除夜の鐘を聴いて、初詣に出かける……という日本のよくある年末年始の風景には、キリスト教＆仏教＆神道がミックスされています。
2月になれば、日本中で豆まきをして、日本中でバレンタインデーを楽しんでいるし、教会で結婚式を挙げ、葬式にはお寺を使い、お祭りには神社の縁日にも行くし、ハロウィンだって、もちろん楽しみます。

The Japanese ethos takes well to appropriating the best parts of other cultures.
Over the New-Year's season, people celebrate Christmas, ring out the mortal sins at a temple, then pray for the new year at a shrine. Christianity, Buddhism and Shinto coexist without friction.
Come February, people around the country drive demons from their houses by throwing beans, then jovially celebrate Valentine's Day the next week. People get wed in a church, have funerals at a temple, and enjoy festivals at a shrine. In recent years, you can even see crowds dressed up for Halloween.

日本の文化も残しながら、西洋の文化も取り入れる。
古い歴史を保ちながら、新しい技術も否定しない。
古いものと新しいもの、東洋的なものと西洋的なもの、自然なものと人工的なものとがコラボレーションする。
「いいものはいい」と、「いいとこどり」して、楽しみながら生きる。
「やおよろず」の神様を持つ日本は、どこもカラフルで柔軟な国だと思います。

Western culture has been adopted alongside the ancient traditions of Japan.
New technology is welcomed while staying true to history.
New and old. Eastern and Western. Natural and artificial. In Japan, these contrasting elements coexist in harmony.
Good things are good, so why not adopt them for a better life?
The country of eight million gods is rich in color and surprisingly flexible.

SPECIALITY ③

日本人は、4種類の文字を使い分けて、豊かに表現します。そして、世界中で使われている絵文字は、日本発祥です。

４つの文字を使い分ける国

FOUR ALPHABETS

Four different types of characters are used in written Japanese, allowing an astoundingly rich variety of expression.
Japan also gave birth to the emoji boom which has taken the world by storm.

舞	山	太	海	春	か	啓	桜	空	木
を	日	来	ピ	令	米	ヅ	イ	あ	ミ
月	大	金	え	気	ヲ	湖	祭	丸	今
せ	い	で	ン	清	ぷ	鳥	歌	わ	雨
踊	夏	の	風	本	冬	思	ゑ	土	火
佳	五	お	げ	伎	強	魂	ヒ	さ	か
和	陽	地	川	よ	氏	り	田	元	秋

©NTT DOCOMO, INC.
ニューヨーク近代美術館(MoMA)に収蔵された絵文字

ばばただざかやぁあわらやまはなたさか あ
びびぢじぎっいぬりゆみひにちしきい
ぶぶづすぐゅう ゑるよむふぬつすくう
ぺべでぜげょえをれ　めへねでせけえ
ぼほどぞごわおんろ　もほのとそこお

ア イ ウ エ オ カ キ ク ケ コ
サ シ ス セ ソ タ チ ツ テ ト
ナ ニ ヌ ネ ノ ハ ヒ フ ヘ ホ
マ ミ ム メ モ ヤ ゐ ユ ゑ ヨ
ラ リ ル レ ロ ワ ヰ ン

0 1 2 3 4 5 6 7 8 9

A B C D E F G H I J K L M N

O P Q R S T U V W X Y Z

a b c d e f g h i j k l m n

o p q r s t u v w x y z

亜哀愛悪握圧扱安案暗以衣位囲医依委威胃為尉異移偉意違維慰遺緯域育一壱逸芋引印因姻員

陰陰飲隠韻右宇羽雨運雲永泳英映栄営詠影鋭衛易疫益液駅悦越謁閲円延沿炎宴援園煙猿遠鉛

演縁汚王凹央応往押欧殴桜翁奥横屋億虞乙卸音恩温穏下化火加可仮何花佳価果河科架夏家花

菓貨渦過嫁暇禍靴寡歌箇稼課蚊我画芽賀雅餓介回灰会快戒改怪拐悔海界皆械絵開階解塊壊懐

日本の文字は、漢字・カタカナ・ひらがな・ローマ字の4種類があり（算用数字を別の文字とみなせば5種類）、日本人はそれらを器用に使い分け、混ぜ合わせることで、想いや心、そして世界を、非常に豊かに表現しています。

In Japan, four types of written characters are used in daily life. *Kanji* are logographic characters derived from Chinese, while *hiragana* and *katakana* are phonetic alphabets unique to Japan. In addition to these three, the Roman alphabet is also widely used. Japanese people adeptly interchange between these four types of characters, mixing and matching to enable them to richly and specifically portray their thoughts, feelings and world view.

人 [hito] [jin] [nin]

漢字は、現代で使われている文字の中で最古の文字体系であり、かつ、人類史上で最も文字数が多く、その数は10万字を軽く超えて、他の文字体系を圧倒しています。ちなみに日本人は、学校で1945字の常用漢字を学び、一般的には約3000字の漢字を読めると言われています。

さらに、日本語の特徴としては、基本的に1つの漢字に最低2つの読み方があります。例えば「人」という漢字は、中国語では「れん (ren)」と発音しますが、日本語では「じん (JIN)」とも言うし「ひと (HITO)」とも言います。

Kanji are one of the oldest script types still in use. They are also one of the most complicated "alphabets" with characters numbering over 100,000, far greater than any other alphabet. Japanese must learn 1,945 of these at school, and generally use around 3,000 of them in daily life. Another distinct feature of Japanese is that each kanji can usually be read in two or more ways. Take, for example, the *kanji* "人". In Chinese it is read as '*ren*,' but in Japanese it can be read as '*jin*' or '*hito*,' depending on the context.

心 [kokoro] [shin]

　ゴロゴロ、ドンドン、つるつる、キラキラ、ぐちゃぐちゃ……など、擬音語、擬態語、擬声語、擬容語、擬情語が日本語にはたくさんあります。これは他の言語の表現に比べると数十倍はあるのです。例えば「ゴロゴロ」という言葉。「カミナリがゴロゴロなる」は擬音語、「岩がゴロゴロ転がる」は擬態語、「猫がノドをゴロゴロならす」は擬声語、「休みの日はゴロゴロしている」は擬容語、「目にゴミが入ってゴロゴロする」は擬情語です。

　ひとつの語がたくさんの意味と用法を持ち、音だけで状態や雰囲気までを表現できるのが日本語なのです。

Japanese is also rich in onomatopoeia and imitative words, with several dozen times more onomatopoeic words in use than other languages. The term 'gorogoro' can express the sound of thunder, the way a rock tumbles, the voice of a purring cat, the state of slumber on a Sunday morning, or the feeling of discomfort when you have something in your eye.
In Japanese, a single word can have numerous meanings and be used in various ways, enabling a rich variety of expressions.

現在、世界中の人々のコミュニケーションに欠かせないものとなっている「絵文字(emoji)」は、日本から世界に広まりました。
世界で初めて携帯電話からインターネット通信が可能なiモードが登場したときに、絵文字が生まれたのです。のちに、このときに生まれた最初の絵文字 176個が、ニューヨーク近代美術館(MoMA)で常設収蔵されることになり、大きな話題となりました。
世界には「emoji」の由来は「emo(tion)」+「ji(字)」と思っている人もいますが、実は日本の「絵文字」なのです。

The emoji that have now become an indispensable form of communication around the world originated in Japan back when the first mobile phones were connected to the Internet. 176 of the very first emoji are now housed in the Museum of Modern Art in New York. While it is often thought that the term emoji comes from a combination of the words 'emotion' + '*ji*' (character), in reality it is borrowed from the Japanese kanji 絵文字 meaning 'picture character'.

日本は、世界最長寿の国です。
人間の寿命だけでなく、世界有数の長寿な企業、
世界最古の歴史を持つ文化なども多数あります。

SPECIALITY ④

長 寿 の 国

LONGEVITY

Japan is known as the land of longevity.
While longevity is usually associated with human life,
Japan also has some of the longest running corporations and oldest cultural assets
as well.

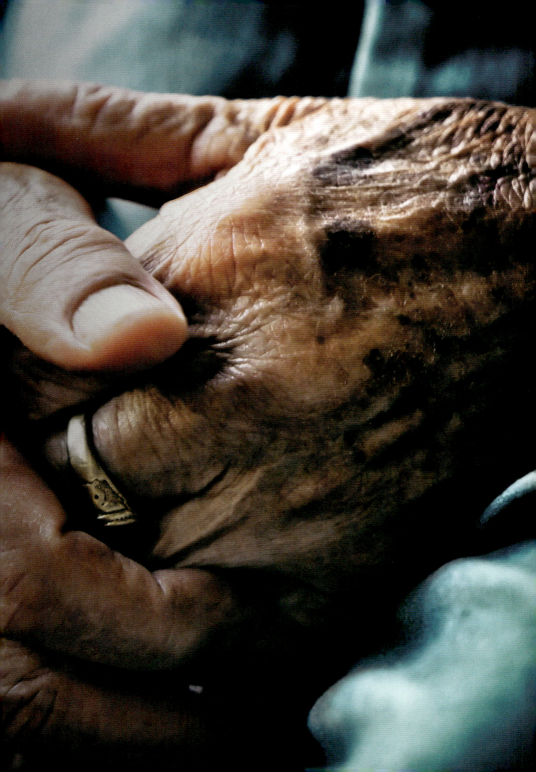

できることなら健康で長生きしたいというのは世界の人類共通の願い。2016年5月のWHOの発表によると、2015年の日本人の平均寿命は83.7歳で、世界で第1位でした。男女別で見ても、80.5歳だった男性については世界6位でしたが、女性は86.8歳でみごと世界ナンバーワン。日本は20年以上前から長寿世界一の座を守り続けています。また、2015年に惜しくも亡くなられてしまいましたが、日本人女性の大川ミサヲさんは114歳の時点で世界最高齢としてギネス世界記録登録され、117歳まで元気に暮らしました。

Longevity is a common wish for people the world over. According the WHO, at 83.7 years, average life expectancy in Japan was top in the world, a position it has maintained for over 20 years. While at an average 80.5 years men in Japan are number six in the world, women are the longest living at an average of 86.8 years. While she has since sadly passed away, Misawo Ohkawa was recognized by Guinness as the oldest living person in the world at age 114. She went on to live happily to 117 years of age!

日本人が長寿である理由は、主に、以下の4つだと考えられています。
医療機関、保険制度の充実。
多様性に富み、バランスのいい食事。
清潔好きな国民性と公衆衛生が高いレベルで保たれていること。
民族的な遺伝的要素。
その他には、入浴の習慣、健康保健教育の充実、退職後の社会参加率の高さ、などを指摘する研究もあります。

Longevity in Japan is attributed to the following four reasons.
Well-developed healthcare services and health insurance
A varied and balanced diet
A high standard of public hygiene and love of cleanliness
Ethnic genetic predisposition
Research also points to other factors contributing to longevity such as bathing customs, health education, and a high rate of participation in society for the elderly.

日本では、人間の寿命だけではなく、企業も長寿です。
創業100年を超える法人が、全国で2万社以上あり、なんと、創業1000年を超える法人が8社あります。
ちなみに、日本最高齢の会社は飛鳥時代(578年)に創業された寺社建築の企業。年齢1441歳。

日本人は、世代を超えて、文化を、しきたりを、想いを伝えていきます。

Humans are not the only ones boasting longevity in Japan. There are some 20,000 companies in operation today that were founded more than 100 years ago, and eight companies whose origins date back more than 1,000 years!
The oldest company in Japan is a temple construction company which was founded in the

日本には、「世界最古」の歴史を持つ文化がたくさんあります。
平安時代に書かれた「源氏物語」は、世界最古の長編小説。
「万葉集」は1500年の歴史を持つ、世界最古の歌集。
「法隆寺」は1400年の歴史がある、世界最古の木造建築物。
「雅楽」は1200年以上続く、世界最古の宮廷音楽。
「能・狂言」は600年以上継承されている、世界最古の演劇。

ちなみに、世界最古の宿も、日本にあることをごぞんじでしょうか?
2011年にギネス世界記録に認定されている山梨県にある、慶雲館です。
慶雲館は文武天皇の慶雲2年、西暦705年が起源とされており1300年以上もの
間、営業しています。

Japan lays claim to numerous other 'oldest' world records too.
'*Genjii Monogatari*' (The Tale of Genji) from the Heian Period is considered to be the
world's oldest novel.
'*Manyoshu*' is the world's oldest extant collection of poems dating back 1,500 years.
'*Horyuji*' is the world's oldest wooden building dating back 1,400 years.
'*Gagaku*' is the world's oldest imperial court music dating back 1,200 years.
'*Noh*' and '*Kyogen*' are the world's oldest theatrical performances having been passed
down for over 600 years.

Did you know that the world's oldest hotel is also in Japan? Having been in operation for
over 1,300 years since its establishment in 705AD, Keiunkan in Yamanashi Prefecture was
recognized by Guinness in 2011.

SPECIALITY:4　43

治安が良く、安心して暮らせる国であることも、日本の特徴のひとつです。

犯罪率も、失業率も、世界最小レベルであり、世界有数の警察力を持ちます。

さらに、公共施設の衛生面、移動手段の時間の正確さにおいても、世界トップクラスの評価を得ています。

SPECIALITY ❺

安 心 ＆ 安 全 な 国

SAFETY &
PEACE

Japan is world renowned for its peace and security.
Crime and unemployment are amongst the lowest in the world,
and the country boasts a powerful police force.
Public facilities are known for their cleanliness,
and the punctuality of public transportation is unmatched around the world.

2017年、英国の雑誌『エコノミスト』が発表した、「世界の安全な都市ランキング」によると、世界の都市の中で、トップは東京。そして、3位に大阪がランクインしました。(ちなみに、2位はシンガポール)。

これは、世界60都市を対象に、主に、「サイバーセキュリティ」「医療・健康環境の安全性」「インフラの安全性」「個人の安全性」という4つの視点で評価したもので、世界的に見ても、日本の各都市の安全度が際立つ結果となりました。

According to a 2017 report by British magazine *The Economist*, Tokyo is the safest city in the world, while Osaka ranked third (second was Singapore).
The report ranked 60 cities based on digital security, health security, infrastructure security and personal security. All cities around Japan boast a high level of safety.

人口10万人あたりの殺人件数は、1年間で0.4件。
これは、世界194の国と地域を対象とした調査で、ルクセンブルクに続いて、世界第2位の少なさになります。(出典:世界保健機関 / WHO 2012年)
殺人事件の解決率においても、日本 (95.9%)・アメリカ (68.3%)・メキシコ (2%) などの統計データを見てもわかるように、世界トップクラスの警察力を持っています。

The annual homicide rate in Japan is just 0.4/100,000.
Of the 194 countries surveyed, this is second only to Luxembourg. (Source: WHO 2012)
In Japan 95.5% of murder cases are solved, in contrast to 68.8% in the USA, and just 2% in Mexico, illustrating the effectiveness of the police force in Japan.

日本の失業率は世界的に見ると非常に低く、欧米の先進国を中心とするOECD諸国34カ国中33位。
日本の失業率は2014年のデータによると3.6％。
加盟国の平均が10.3％、アメリカが6.1％なので、主要な国と比べてみても日本の失業率がいかに低いかがわかります。ちなみに1位のギリシャは26.3％です。
この失業率の低さも、治安が維持されている原因のひとつとされています。

The unemployment rate in Japan is extremely low, at 33rd of 34 OECD countries. As of 2014 the official unemployment rate in Japan was 3.6% compared to an average of 10.3%, and 6.1% in the USA. Unemployment in the OECD topped at 26.3% in Greece. Low unemployment is thought to be one of the leading factors in maintaining public security.

第二次大戦後に、世界的に例を見ない速度で、経済を発展させた国、日本。面積は小さな国ですが、2019年現在、経済の規模においては、アメリカ、中国に続いて、世界第3位のGDPを持つ、世界有数の経済大国です。

SPECIALITY ❻

戦後に驚異的な経済成長を遂げた国

ECONOMIC GROWTH

Following WWII, Japan set about rebuilding the devastated country, achieving economic growth at a rate never seen before across the globe. While the country may be small in size, it is grand in economic scale, with the GDP ranking third in the world behind the USA and China.

第二次世界大戦で、一度は、焼け野原のようになってしまった日本ですが、戦後の復興期を経て、高度経済成長と呼ばれる期間 (1955 〜 1973年) では、実質経済成長率で年率10 〜 20%もの凄まじい経済成長を遂げました。
世界銀行によると、経済の規模を表す数字であるGDPが、1954年から1973年の19年間で、約10倍に拡大しました。そして、1968年には、アメリカに次ぐ世界第2位の経済大国になりました。

During WWII, large areas of Japan were burnt to the ground. Reconstruction efforts bolstered the economy, with growth rates at a stunning 10-20% per annum through the years 1955 – 1973.
According to the World Bank, GDP increased tenfold during the years 1954 to 1973. By 1968, Japan had become the world's second economic superpower, behind only the USA.

戦後、焼け野原で何もないところから、たった約20年の間に、世界第2位の経済大国まで上り詰めたというのは世界的に見ても例がなく、第二次大戦終戦直後の復興から続く一連の経済成長は「東洋の奇跡」(英語では「Japanese miracle」)と言われました。
この驚異的な経済成長への憧れや敬意から、東南アジア諸国を中心に、日本をモデルとする国が、多く現れました。

Japan rebuilt from the ashes of war, creating an economy that ranked second in the world in just 20 years. This unmatched growth has been nicknamed the 'Japanese miracle' and later inspired other countries, especially in southeast Asia, to look to Japan as a model for growth.

その後、もちろん、景気の波はありましたが、現在（2019年）でも、日本は、アメリカ、中国に次いで、世界第3位のGDPを持ち、世界有数の経済規模を持つ国です。

ただし、発展途上国への総合的な貢献度を測る「発展途上国支援ランキング」（The Commitment to Development Index / 2015）では、先進国27ヵ国中で最下位になるなど、国際社会への貢献度が高いとは決して言えません。

そして、国内でも、経済を優先するあまりに引き起こしてきた環境汚染、公害と言われる病気の問題、原子力発電所の安全管理、過疎化の問題など、多くの問題を抱えています。

21世紀の現在、国境を越えて世界中の国々とフレンドシップを築きながら、経済発展の先にある新しいビジョンを描いていくことが、期待されていると思います。

While the Japanese economy has seen its share of ups and downs in recent years, still today in 2019 it maintains its place as third in the world for GDP. On the other hand, Japan ranks lowest of 27 countries covered in the 'Commitment to Development index 2015', which assesses a country's overall commitment to supporting developing nations, highlighting a lack of contribution to global society.

Domestically too the focus on economic growth has caused environmental destruction, sicknesses from pollution, negligence of safety measures at nuclear power plants, depopulation of rural areas, and a host of other issues.

In the 21st-century, we must reach out across borders, foster friendship and create a new vision of what to pursue as the next step following economic growth.

1945年8月。広島・長崎。
日本は、世界で唯一、
原爆投下によって被爆した国です。
その経験を受けて、
世界でも例を見ない平和憲法を持つ国になりました。
現在も、世界の平和な国ランキングでは、
常にトップ10内に入る国ですが、同時に、
世界第8位の軍事費を持つ軍事大国でもあります。

SPECIALITY ❼

世界唯一の被爆国であり、平和憲法のある国

ATOMIC BOMB & PEACE CONSTITUTION

Hiroshima. Nagasaki. In August 1945, Japan became the only country in the world to suffer the wrath of an atomic bombing. This experience lead to the creation of a Peace Constitution, giving Japan a truly unique position in the world. While Japan has consistently ranked in the top ten peaceful countries in the world, it maintains a heavily armed Self Defense Force with military spending eighth in the world.

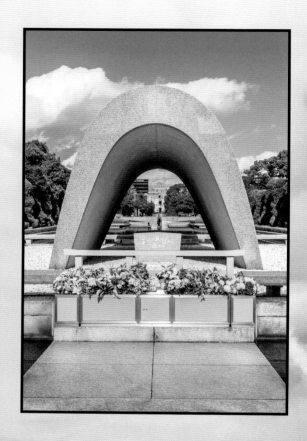

1945年8月に、人類史上初めて、広島・長崎に、原子爆弾が投下されました。その年だけで、合計約21万人の方が亡くなり、16万人の方が重軽傷を負いました。核のない世界への祈りとして、広島市にある原爆死没者慰霊碑には、「安らかに眠って下さい　過ちは繰返しませぬから」という言葉が刻まれています。

In August 1945, the first atomic bombs were dropped on Hiroshima and Nagasaki cities, killing around 210,000 people in that year alone and injuring 160,000 more. As a prayer for a world without nuclear weapons, a plaque on the cenotaph for A-bomb victims in Hiroshima reads, 'Let all the souls here rest in peace, for we will not repeat the evil.'

戦争の悲劇を胸に、日本は、人類の財産とまで言われる、平和憲法を持つ国になりました。
愛と平和を大切にして、戦争はしない。軍隊も持たない。
まるで、ジョン・レノンの歌のような憲法です。
以下、条文になります。

『日本国憲法 第九条』

日本国民は、正義と秩序を基調とする国際平和を誠実に希求し、

国権の発動たる戦争と、武力による威嚇又は武力の行使は、

国際紛争を解決する手段としては、永久にこれを放棄する。

前項の目的を達するため、陸海空軍その他の戦力は、これを保持しない。

国の交戦権は、これを認めない。

With the scars of war barely healed, Japan adopted a Peace Constitution that has become a model for the world.
Foster love and peace. Renounce war. Maintain no military.
A constitution that is reminiscent of a certain John Lennon song.
Here is an article from Japan's constitution.

[Article 9 of the Constitution of Japan]
Aspiring sincerely to an international peace based on justice and order, the Japanese people forever renounce war as a sovereign right of the nation and the threat or use of force as means of settling international disputes.
In order to accomplish the aim of the preceding paragraph, land, sea, and air forces, as well as other war potential, will never be maintained. The right of belligerency of the state will not be recognized.

日本は、素晴らしい平和憲法を掲げる国でありながら、現実的には、世界第8位の軍事予算を持つ、軍事大国でもあります。(出典:ストックホルム国際平和研究所 2017)
「軍隊」とは呼びませんが、総員20万人を超える「自衛隊」が存在し、「軍事費」とは呼びませんが、年間5兆円を超える「防衛費」が、毎年、使われています。
2018年に行われた世論調査では、18歳以上の国民の約7割が、「憲法九条を評価する」と答えていますが、憲法改正を求める意見も多くあり、現在も議論が続いています。(出典: NHK世論調査 憲法に関する意識調査2018)

Despite Japan's wonderful Peace Constitution, it still has the eighth largest military (defense) budget in the world. (Source: Stockholm International Peace Research Institute 2017)
While it is not called a military by name, Japan's Self Defense Forces number 200,000 personnel, and the annual defense budget, while not strictly a 'military' budget, is in excess of 5 trillion yen.
While a survey of public opinion in 2018 showed around 70% of Japanese over 18 supported Article 9 of the constitution, there is also a not-insignificant minority who want to change it, resulting in ongoing debate. (Source: NHK Opinion Poll 2018)

和

Wa

SPECIALITY 8

感 謝 の 国

DAILY
APPRECIATION

In Japan, feelings of appreciation are contained in everyday greetings,
reflecting the spirit of 'wa' (harmony) that has been passed down since ancient times.

日本語の日常の挨拶には、感謝の気持ちが含まれています。日本には、古くから受け継がれてきた、「和」の精神があります。

ありがとうございます。

おめでとうございます。

いただきます。

ごちそうさまでした。

ごめんください。

ごめんなさい。

こちらこそ。

さようなら。

こんばんは。

いってきます。

いってらっしゃい。

おかえりなさい。

ただいま。

日本の挨拶というのは、感謝と愛情が込められている独自の言葉です。

例えば、毎回の食事の前後に言う、「いただきます」「ごちそうさま」。
これは、料理を作ってくれた人、食材を生産してくれた人、深くは、命への敬意を
表す挨拶で、他国の言葉に翻訳できません。
「いってらっしゃい」という挨拶には、「気をつけて」「頑張ってね」というニュアン
スが含まれていますし、「ただいま」と言うだけで、「元気に戻ったよ」というニュ
アンスが含まれています。「おかえり」の一言にも、「無事で帰ってきて嬉しい」「お
つかれさま」というニュアンスが含まれています。

「ただいま」は、英語に直訳すると、「JUST NOW」。
「おかえり」は、「WELCOME BACK」。
英語に直訳すると、ほとんど意味を成さない、日本独特の表現です。

日本人は、「I LOVE YOU」という表現を、日常的にはあまり使いませんが、
それは、普段の挨拶の中に、もう、それが含まれているからかもしれません。
言葉の奥に、「喜び・感謝・祈り・愛」のようなものを込めて、さりげなく伝える。
それが、日本語の美しさです。

The Japanese have special greeting words that contain nuances of appreciation and love.

Before and after meals, Japanese say 'itadakimasu' and 'gochisosama,' two words that
are difficult to translate but show appreciation to the food, the people who grew the food,
the people who cooked the food, and to life (food) itself.
'Itterashai,' said to someone leaving the house, is literally translated as "off you go," but
contains feelings of "take care" and "do your best."
'Tadaima,' said when you arrive home, is literally translated as "just now," but also means
"I arrived home safely."
'Okaeri,' said to someone who just got home, is literally translated as "you're home," but
contains feelings of '"welcome back" and "you must be tired."
In this way, the translations into other languages do not do justice to the true meanings
behind these common Japanese greetings.

It is well known that the Japanese do not often say "I love you," but that may be due in part
to the fact that this feeling is already portrayed in their everyday greetings.
Hidden in these simple greetings are feelings of joy, appreciation, prayer and love.
This subtle form of expression is part of what makes Japan so beautiful.

しつれいしました。
すみません。
おげんきで。
おだいじに。
おねがいします。
お待たせいたしました。
では、また。
どういたしまして。
おはようございます。
おやすみなさい。
はじめまして。
かしこまりました。
どうぞよろしく。

SPECIALITY:8

和の心〜SPIRIT OF "WA"〜

2013年には和食が、2014年には和紙が世界文化遺産に登録され、最近、「和」の文化が、あらためて、世界で注目されています。
「和」というのは、中国の歴史書『魏志倭人伝』に出てくる言葉で、「日本」を指す言葉です。「和」には、Japanese styleの他に、soften（和らげる）、relax（和む）、harmony（調和する）、peace（平和）などの意味があります。

日本人は、国際的な比較で、ときに、「自分がない」「自己主張しない」「優柔不断」などと言われることもありますが、きっと、そうではなくて。
全体が和み、調和して、平和な空気になれるように……。
そんな、「和」の心を、大切にしているのだと思います。

In 2013 *washoku* was designated as a World Cultural Heritage, followed by *washi* in 2014. This shows a renewed appreciation for the '*wa*' culture of Japan.
A phrase in the Chinese history book *Sanguozhi* refers to Japan as '*wa*.' However, the kanji "和" (*wa*) has a broad range of meanings. Other than the common 'Japanese style,' it can also mean 'soften,' 'relax,' 'harmony' and 'peace'.

Compared with other cultures, Japanese are often said to lack self-assertion, have no opinion, or be indecisive.
Rather than being a negative trait, I think this is a reflection of appreciation for harmony and peace, which Japanese value above self-assertion.

和らげる
和む
調和する
平和

TREASURE

世界に誇る日本の宝物

日本発祥の面白いモノを紹介

Treasures and interesting innovations from Japan

さて、ここからは、日本のモノを見てみましょう。

日本には、世界中の多くの人から愛されるユニークな商品や習慣がたくさんあります。
そして、日本発祥で、世界の流行やスタンダードになっているものも、少なくありません。

日本に暮らしていると、あたりまえのことだけど、
海外の人から見ると、感動と衝撃の体験……。

そんな、日本ならではの「宝物」を厳選して、
いくつか紹介します。

Let's now take a look at some interesting ideas and products that originated in Japan.
There are many unique Japanese products and customs that have gained popularity around the world. As such, many of these things have come to be considered a global standard.
Living in Japan, it's easy to take these global treasures for granted. Sometimes it helps to take a step back and reevaluate them. Here are some of our favorites.

TREASURE 1

温水洗浄便座
SPRAY TOILET SEATS

This amazing appliance with technology comparable with that aboard the Hayabusa asteroid probe has become one of the symbols of Japan.

日本を代表する、世界が羨む生活用品。小惑星探査機「はやぶさ」搭載のテクノロジーにも匹敵する、水を操る技術。

1

日本には素晴らしいものがたくさんありますが、その中でも、来日した外国の人たちが最も絶賛するのが、快適で清潔な温水洗浄便座なのです。
快適な温水シャワーでお尻を洗ってくれる「シャワー機能」と、座るとじわっと温かい「暖房便座」は、日本ではどこに行ってもあたりまえにありますが、海外のトイレにはほとんどないので、日本を訪れる外国人観光客の多くが「これはすごい！ 快適だ！」と驚きます。

世界のポップスター、マドンナが12年ぶりに来日した際には、「あの温かい便座が、ずっと恋しかったの」と言った、というエピソードも残っています。

Japan has many great appliances, but the one that gets overseas visitors the most excited is the spray toilet seat.
These electronic wonders with warm seats and warm water sprays to wash your bottom are ubiquitous in Japan, but can rarely be found in other countries, which is why visitors to Japan are so surprised by how pleasant and comfortable they are.

In 2005 visiting pop superstar Madonna reportedly commented that she 'missed Japan's warm toilet seats.'

もともと温水洗浄便座は、欧米で開発された医療・福祉向けの製品でした。それを日本メーカーが輸入して販売していたのですが、その後、独自開発を進め、様々なテクノロジーを搭載して1960年代後半から国内生産が始まりました。

「ウォシュレット」はTOTO株式会社の登録商標で、他社では「シャワートイレ」や「ビューティ・トワレ」と呼ばれる商品などがあります。

ちなみに「ウォシュレット」は、「Let's Wash（さあ、洗いましょう！）」を逆にして生まれたそうです。

Toilets with warm water spray were actually first developed in the west for use in medical and nursing applications. The idea caught on in Japan, with domestic production beginning in the late 1960s incorporating a variety of technological advancements.

The term *'Washlet'* (a play on the words 'let's wash') was popularized by market leader TOTO, while other companies came up with their own versions such as the *'Shower Toilet'* and *'Beauty Toilette.'*

TREASURE:1 73

日本メーカーが競い合って磨いてきたシャワー機能には様々なテクノロジーが搭載されています。
「ウォシュレット」のTOTOは、少ない温水でもしっかりとした洗い心地のあるシャワーをとことん追求し続け、「エアインワンダーウェーブ洗浄」という技術を開発しました。

Toilet seats developed through competition between Japanese manufacturers contain a startling array of advanced technology. Let's take a look at some of the secrets to their success. TOTO has committed to water-saving features for their spray seat which have led to the *'Wonder-Wave Cleansing'* technology.

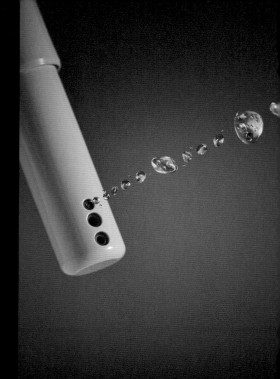

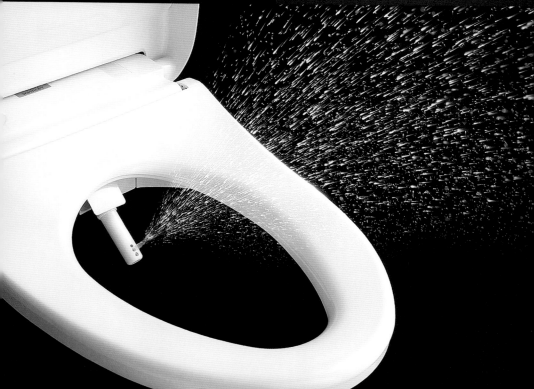

噴射される温水には秘密が満載です。まず、シャワー水流のスピードを周期的に変化させることで、先に出た遅い水に後から出た速い水が追いついて大きな水玉がつくられています。その水玉は、なんと1秒間に約100個噴射され、少ない水量でパワフルな洗浄力を実現しているのです。さらに、その噴射する水玉に空気を含ませることで、水の一粒一粒を約30％拡大し、たっぷりとした洗い心地を実現しています。
ちなみに、ノズルから噴出する温水の角度は43度。これはお尻に当たって跳ね返ってくる温水がノズルを汚さないように計算されているのです。

The technology sends 'waves' of slower and faster water which overlap to create large droplets. Around 100 of these droplets are sprayed every second, enabling a powerful spray using just a little water. Additionally, the droplets are injected with air, making them around 30% larger, yet again increasing their cleansing power. Water from the nozzle is aimed up at 43 degrees, an angle calculated so spray reflected from your bottom doesn't drip back and dirty the nozzle.

この水を操る技術は、電動の小型ポンプをつかっているため、高級な「ウォシュレット」に搭載されています。TOTOの技術者は、普及価格帯の「ウォシュレット」にも水玉連射のシャワーを搭載したいと考えました。価格を抑えるためには、ポンプは使えません。そこで思いついたのは、シャワーの通り道に小部屋をつくり、その小部屋を「水」と「空気」で交互に満たす仕組み、「バルーンジェット技術」でした。シャワーが流れると、小部屋の中に大きな空気の泡が次々と発生するため、シャワーが泡を通るときはそのままのスピード、泡がないときは水の抵抗を受けるのでスピードが遅くなります。その結果、シャワーのスピードが周期的に変化するため、ポンプを使わなくても水玉連射が実現しました。

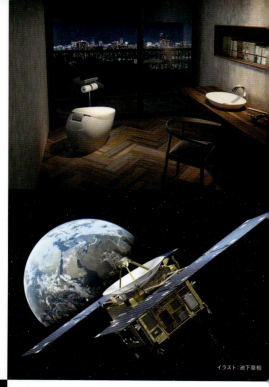

イラスト：池下章裕

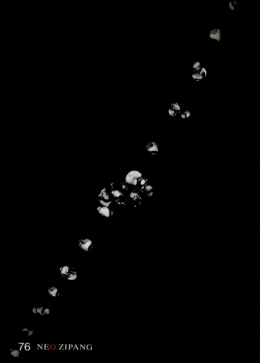

This aquatic technological wonder is made possible with a miniature water pump installed in high-end models. Developers at TOTO wanted to incorporate the washing technology into mid-range models but needed a way around the expensive pumps. They eventually came up with the 'balloon jet' which fills a small chamber in the water supply pipe alternately with water and air. When water passes through the empty chamber, it comes out at full speed, and when the chamber is full, the water slows, resulting in a wave-like pattern of large droplets without the need for a pump.

流体力学を駆使して水と空気の"流れ"を高度に操り、不安定な大きな泡を安定的に生み出す技術が高く評価されて、小惑星探査機「はやぶさ」搭載の流体力学テクノロジーと同じ賞を受賞しています。温水洗浄便座に高度な流体力学テクノロジーを搭載する、日本の技術者のこだわりこそが、これからも日本のものづくりを支えていくことでしょう。

This understanding of hydrodynamics, managing the flow of water and air to create a stable flow of 'unstable' large droplets was so revolutionary that it won the technology prize from the Japan Society of Fluid Mechanics, the same prize that was awarded to technology aboard the Hayabusa asteroid probe.
This passion for pursuing top-end products incorporating cutting edge hydrodynamics in toilet spray seats is exactly what will keep Japan as a leader in technology and development of exciting new products.

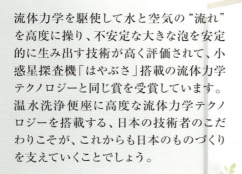

人口29人あたり1台！　年間総売上額は約5兆円！　世界一の自動販売機大国・日本では、温かい物も冷たい物も、おもちゃもお守りも焼きたてピザも、いつでもどこでも買え、さらには、困った人を助ける機能まで搭載し始めています。

TREASURE ②

自動販売機
VENDING MACHINES

One vending machine for every 29 people in Japan! Global sales of 5 trillion yen! Japan is the world leader in vending machines, offering warm and cold drinks, toys, amulets, and even hot pizza anytime, anywhere. Some vending machines now even come with functions to help people in emergencies.

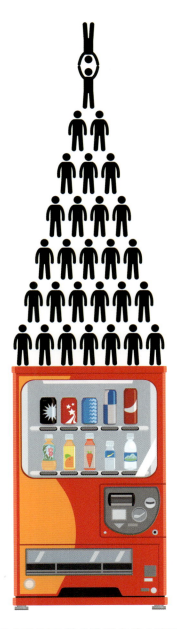

日本国内の自動販売機の設置台数427万1,400台
これは日本の人口**29人あたり1台**
（2017年末時点・日本自動販売システム機械工業会調べ）

日本には、無人でものを売る機械「自動販売機」は、427万1,400台あります。そのうち飲み物の販売機は244万3,800台です（2017年末時点・日本自動販売システム機械工業会調べ）。これは日本の人口29人あたり1台ある計算になります。

1人あたりの設置台数はダントツの世界一で、自動販売機の年間総売上額も約5兆円あります。これは普及台数世界一のアメリカの売上金額を超えていて、世界一の自動販売機大国と呼ばれています。

There are some 4,271,400 automated vending machines in Japan, of which 2,443,800 sell drinks (according to a 2017 survey by the Japan Vending System Manufacturers Association). With a population of around 120 million, this means there is one vending machine for every 29 people in Japan, by far the highest number per capita in the world. Though the USA may have more vending machines in operation, with gross annual sales reaching 5 trillion yen, Japan is known as the vending machine leader of the world.

外国人の方々が日本に来て驚くのが、自動販売機が「どこにでもある」ことです。

他の国では駅や商業施設の中にしか置いてありません。日本のように、屋外や、交通量や人の行き来が少ない場所に設置されることはほとんどありえないのです。

理由は、そういう場所に置くと、壊されたり、自動販売機ごと盗まれたりしてしまうから。鉄格子で囲まれた自動販売機があるほどです。

自動販売機がどこにでもあるということは、治安の良さ、素晴らしさの証なのです。

ホットコーヒー、アイスティ、ジュース、お水、栄養ドリンクなど、バラエティ豊かな商品が一緒に売られているのは、世界広しと言えども、日本以外にはありません。特に冷たい飲み物と温かい飲み物が同じ機械で買えるということは、日本特有の驚くべきことです。
これは、世界に誇れる日本のものづくり精神、そして高い技術力があってこそ、なのです。

Vending machines in Japan also boast a huge range of products sold in one machine, from hot coffee to iced tea, juices, water, and energy drinks. Another surprising fact is that hot and cold drinks are sold from the same vending machine, a feat made possible by advanced Japanese technology and ingenuity.

What surprises visitors to Japan the most is the prevalence of vending machines just about everywhere they go. In most countries, vending machines are usually only installed in train stations or commercial facilities, and almost never outdoors or in areas with little traffic. The main reason for this is to prevent vandalism or theft. In some countries, vending machines are even encaged in steel bars. The ubiquity of vending machines in Japan is made possible by, and a testament to, a high level of public security.

ホットメニュー自動販売機 / 株式会社ニチレイフーズ
※当自動販売機の新規取り扱いはお受けしておりません

日本には本当にたくさんの種類の自動販売機があります。
ドリンクはもちろん、お菓子、アイス、ラーメン、フライドポテト、たこ焼き、ホットドッグ、焼きおにぎり、ポップコーン、おでんなどの食料品や、下着、ひげそり、傘、子ども用のオムツなどの日用品、さらには、本や新聞、おもちゃ、風船、そして、お守りやおみくじまで。
釣具店の軒先では釣り餌も売っているし、生花を売る販売機は温度・湿度の管理も完璧。名刺を作ってくれるもの、豆から挽いて抽出するコーヒー、ピザをその場で焼き上げてくれる自動販売機もあります。

There is a truly astounding variety of vending machines in Japan.
Aside from the usual drinks, you can buy foods such as snacks, ice-cream, hot noodles, French fries, *takoyaki* (octopus balls), hotdogs, rice balls, popcorn, *oden* (stewed food), commodities such as underwear, shaving razors, umbrellas, diapers, books, newspapers, toys, balloons, amulets and even fortune papers.
Under the eaves of a fishing tackle shop you can find a vending machine selling bait. Elsewhere, vending machines selling real flowers have the temperature and humidity managed perfectly. You can print your own business cards, make fresh coffee from beans ground to order, and even get a pizza baked to perfection, all from Japan's unique vending machines.

ソーラーパネル搭載「ecoる/ソーラー」自動販売機/日本コカ・コーラ株式会社

最新型の自動販売機は、ものを売るだけではありません。

心臓の病気で倒れた人の命を救うための自動体外式除細動器（AED）を搭載したものや、公衆無線LANアクセスポイントになっているものまであります。

災害時に、被害を受けた人のために、販売機の中の飲料などを無料で提供する機能を備えたものも登場。さらには、電光掲示板付きの販売機もあり、インターネットを通じてメッセージを発信し、災害時の警報や避難指示を表示するものもあります。

日本の自動販売機は、今も世界トップクラスの進化を遂げ続けているのです。

The latest vending machines are not only for buying things. Some come equipped with AEDs to help save lives in an emergency, and others offer access points for public Wi-Fi. Some vending machines come with a function that dispenses drinks free of charge to people affected by natural disasters. Other vending machines have electric message boards that provide information during disasters, warnings, or evacuation orders. Vending machines in Japan are still evolving at an astonishing rate, staying ahead of the rest of the world.

災害支援型自動販売機/日本コカ・コーラ株式会社

100年以上の歴史を持つ日本発祥の独自アート。食欲をそそる精巧な模型の表現力とアイデアが、世界中を驚かせています。

TREASURE ③

食品サンプル
REPLICA FOOD SAMPLES

A unique art form developed in Japan over 100 years ago.
Elaborate models are made using a unique process to create mouth-watering food replicas.

もともと食品サンプルは、商品の細部や魅力をリアルに伝えるとともに、日本語がわからない外国人でも指差すだけで注文できる便利な販促ツールでした。

しかし現代では、そのリアルでユニークな食品サンプルに感動した外国人旅行者が、日本の観光土産としてこぞって買うようになっています。最近では、キーホルダーやスマホケース、アクセサリーなどといった幅広い商品展開もされ、アートとしての評価も高まっています。

レストランなどの店頭や店内に陳列される料理模型「食品サンプル」は、ビニール樹脂で精巧に作られており、本物の料理以上においしそうに見えます。

この食品サンプル、実は日本発祥の独自文化で、世界中から注目が集まる技術が詰まっているのです。

In Japan, you'll often find replica food samples on display in front of restaurants. These intricate PVC replicas are so well made, they often look tastier that the actual food itself.
Japan has become world renowned for this unique art, with the first wax food samples dating back to the early 1900s.

86　NEO ZIPANG

日本の食品サンプルの歴史は、大正初期の1917年頃に始まったと言われています。その後、1932年に大阪で弁当屋を営んでいた岩崎瀧三が「食品模型岩崎製作所」を創業し、食品サンプルは食の伝道師として大都市から地方都市へ拡大していき、日本中で一般的なものとなりました。日本発祥の食品サンプル文化は、100年以上の歴史を持っているのです。

ちなみに、この岩崎瀧三の故郷である岐阜県の郡上八幡は、食品サンプル発祥の町として発展し、「食品サンプルの町」「食品サンプルの聖地」と呼ばれています。

Replica food samples were originally developed to lure customers with delicious looking food but are also useful for customers who don't speak Japanese. Anyone from anywhere in the world can point to what they want, knowing it is what they will get. Lately however, they have become so popular that you can often find tourists buying them by the dozen as souvenirs. You can buy miniatures to attach to your keys or phone, accessories such as earrings, and a wide range of other novel products. The food replica culture has become a highly regarded artform in and of itself.

The first replica food samples were thought to have been made around 1917, in the early Taisho period. In 1932, the owner of a bento shop in Osaka, Takizo Iwasaki, established a replica food production company. Eventually these food samples spread from large cities to rural towns all over Japan, becoming a common sight over the last century.
Iwasaki's hometown of Gujohachiman in Gifu Prefectures is well known as the birthplace of food samples.

リアルな食品サンプルの中でも特にユニークなのが、「持ち上げ系」と呼ばれるものです。箸やフォークで持ち上げたラーメンやスパゲティ、コーヒーにクリームが注がれているものや、フライパンの上をチャーハンが舞っているもの、さらには寿司を醤油につけようとしているものまであります。
その食欲をそそる表現力やアイデアが、世界を驚かせています。

Especially unique replica food samples show the food mid-meal, with chopsticks lifting *ramen* noodles, spaghetti twirled around a fork, cream being poured into coffee or fried rice being tossed in a wok. You can even see mouth-watering sushi being dipped into soy sauce! These innovative ideas and mouth-watering creations are highly regarded around the world.

The replica food industry in Japan has established itself as a unique aspect of Japanese culture. Many souvenir stores now sell replica food, and you can even take courses in making replicas yourself, which are popular among foreign tourists and Japanese youth alike. There are specialized schools that train people in the art of making plastic replicas. These wonderful creations are a prime example of Japanese delicacy and creativity; a treasure to be shared with the world and future generations.

もはや日本文化のひとつとして確立している食品サンプル業界。お土産を買えるショップはもちろん、実際に製作体験できる工房や、食品サンプル職人を養成するスクールなどもあり、外国人観光客だけではなく、日本の若者の間でも人気が高まっています。日本人の繊細さ、器用さといった素晴らしい部分が凝縮された食品サンプルは、世界に、そして日本の未来にも誇るべき宝なのです。

Information

【食品サンプル百貨店】
メイド・イン・ジャパンの食品サンプル約300点が掲載されたビジュアルブック。

編著：竹村真奈／小西七重
発行：ギャンビット

【元祖食品サンプル屋 合羽橋店】
食品サンプルの父、岩崎瀧三が昭和7年に創業した食品サンプルのリーディングカンパニー株式会社岩崎が運営する食品サンプルの専門店。食品サンプル製作体験をはじめ、ユニークで楽しい商品を見たり買ったりできます。

東京都台東区西浅草3-7-6
つくばエクスプレス「浅草駅」より徒歩5分

公式サイト　https://www.ganso-sample.com/

Book:【Food sample department store】
A visual guide to 300 food samples made in Japan.

Authors: Mana Takemura, Nanae Konishi / Publisher: Gambit

Shop:【Ganso Shokuhin Sample-ya in Kappabashi, Tokyo】
A replica food specialty shop run by leading food sample company Iwasaki, founded by the father of food samples Takizo Iwasaki in 1932. Try making your own replica food and browse or buy from a range of unique and fun products.

Address: 3-7-6 Nishi-Asakusa, Taito-ku, Tokyo
5 minutes on foot from Asakusa Station on the Tsukuba Express Line.

Official website: https://www.ganso-sample.com/

折り紙

紙を折るだけで生み出される偉大なる芸術。折り鶴は世界的な平和の象徴となっており、さらに、折り紙の技法は、世界を変えるかもしれない新たなイノベーションの鍵を握っています。

セルバンテス(2013)

TREASURE ④

ORIGAMI
PAPER FOLDING

This marvelous art form can transform sheets of paper into a myriad of creations. Folded paper cranes have become a symbol of peace worldwide, and the techniques used to make them have led to innovations that have the potential to change the world.

90 NEO ZIPANG

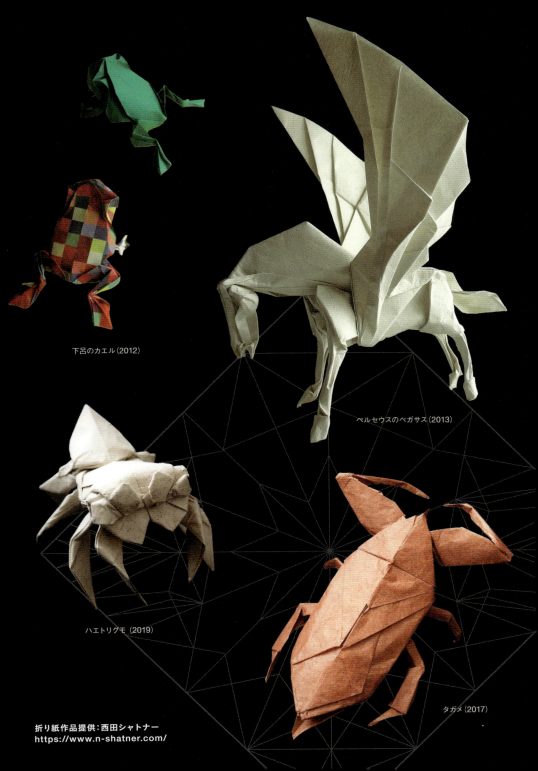

下呂のカエル(2012)
ペルセウスのペガサス(2013)
ハエトリグモ(2019)
タガメ(2017)

折り紙作品提供:西田シャトナー
https://www.n-shatner.com/

ランスロット(2013)

荒川区のT-rex(2012)

紙を折るだけで、鶴やカエルといった動物から、実際に遊ぶことができる飛行機や風船、手裏剣まで、様々な形を作り出す遊び、それが折り紙です。
現在、「折り紙＝ORIGAMI」という言葉は多くの国に浸透し、新しい折り紙作品が世界中あらゆるところで作られ、世界的な作家も多数生まれています。
折り紙は、日本が世界に誇る偉大な芸術なのです。

トンボver.3(2009)

戦う偶蹄類(2013)

クワガタムシver.3(2012)

Origami (lit. 'folding paper') is a traditional Japanese art form that enables you to create anything from animals such as cranes and frogs to toys such as planes, balloons and even ninja stars by folding paper.
The word *origami* has spread to many countries, and there are now famous artists coming up with new origami creations all around the world.
Origami is yet another great art that originated in Japan.

Highly durable Japanese paper known as '*washi*' was developed in the 5th-6th century as a means of keeping records of events. It was later used to wrap offerings to the gods. As people came up with new ways to wrap the offerings beautifully, the art form of origami slowly developed.
People began to enjoy the folding process itself, and origami became a popular pastime during the Edo Period (17th – 19th century). A book published in 1797 '*Hiden Sembazuru Orikata*,' featuring 49 ways to fold paper cranes, is now recognized as the oldest existing book that features origami as a pastime.
Origami is a Japanese art that is said to date back over 400 years.

海亀の子 (2012)

サイ (2008)

大須のトナカイ (2013)

日本では、5〜6世紀頃に薄くて丈夫な紙「和紙」が生まれ、記録するための用紙として使われていました。それから、神様への供物を包むために使われるようになり、「美しく折って包む」ことが流行するようになりました。一説では、この「美しく包む行為」が折り紙の起源だと言われています。
だんだんと折り方そのものを楽しむようになり、江戸時代には「折り紙」が庶民に親しまれるようになりました。1797年には49種類の鶴の折り方が記された『秘傳千羽鶴折形』が出版されています。これが「現存する世界最古の遊戯折り紙の本」と言われています。
折り紙は400年以上の歴史を持つ日本文化と言われています。

TREASURE:4 93

折り紙で作られる鶴、折り鶴は「平和の象徴」としても世界的に知られています。きっかけは、広島で被爆した佐々木禎子さんの話が世界に伝えられたことでした。佐々木禎子さんは2歳のときに被爆し、9年後の小学校6年生のときに白血病と診断され入院しました。それから彼女は回復を願ってお見舞い品の包装紙などを使って鶴を折り続けましたが、闘病生活の甲斐なく12歳で亡くなってしまいました。その直後から、彼女の同級生たちの呼びかけで、平和を築くための像をつくろうという運動が始まり、募金が集まり、広島の平和記念公園内に「原爆の子の像」が完成しました。

この話を、オーストリアの作家カルル・ブルックナーが『Sadako will leben（サダコは生きる）』という本で描き、様々な国で出版されて伝わっていったのです。

「原爆の子の像」には世界中から折り鶴が捧げられて、その数は年間約1千万羽にものぼります。

Paper cranes have become a symbol of peace around the world thanks to the story of Sadako Sasaki, a girl who survived the atomic bombing of Hiroshima when she was two years old. Nine years after the bombing, she was diagnosed with leukemia and hospitalized for treatment. While in the hospital, Sadako would fold paper cranes while wishing for recovery, using wrapping paper from presents people brought her. Sadly, she never recovered, and passed away at age 12. Soon after, her classmates set about creating a movement, collecting donations to erect a statue for peace in her honor. The Children's Peace Monument now stands in Hiroshima Peace Memorial Park.

Hearing this story, Austrian writer Karl Bruckner's book 'Sadako will leben' (Sadako wants to live / English title: The Day of the Bomb) helped spread her story around the world. Paper cranes sent from around the world to the Children's Peace Monument each year number in the tens of millions.

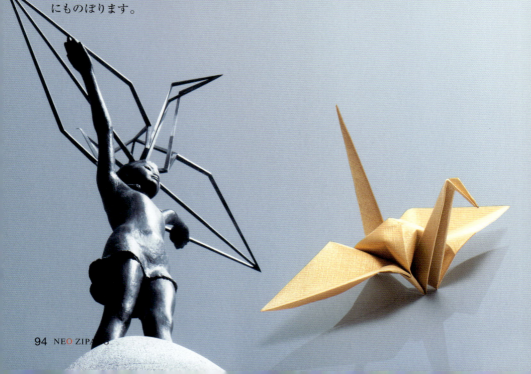

日本の伝統文化である折り紙は、紙から様々な形を作るというだけではなく、近年では、その技術や仕組みを応用して、宇宙をはじめ、あらゆる分野で活用しようという動きが起きています。

有名な例は「ミウラ折り」です。平行四辺形をタイル状に並べた折り目をつけ、山折りと谷折りを繰り返すこの折り方は、端を持って左右に引っ張れば一瞬で広げたり折りたたんだりできます。何度開閉しても破れにくいという利点もあるので、観光マップや地図などにも使われています。ミウラ折りは東京大学名誉教授・文部科学省宇宙科学研究所の三浦公亮さんが、人工衛星の太陽光パネルの自動的に展開する方法を研究しているときに発明されました。以来、今でもNASAの宇宙工学に影響を与え続けているのです。

Lately, techniques and methods of the traditional Japanese art of origami have been adapted to many applications in aerospace and other industries.

One famous example is the *Miura Fold* which is used to fold large, flat surfaces into a small area with repeated mountain-valley folds. The surfaces can then be spread quickly and easily by simply pulling the edges. The folds do not weaken much even with repeated use, making them ideal for folding large sheets such as maps and guides.

The Miura Fold was developed by renowned Japanese astrophysicist Professor Koryo Miura who was researching ways to automatically fold solar panels on satellites. It still plays a part in space engineering even in the NASA program.

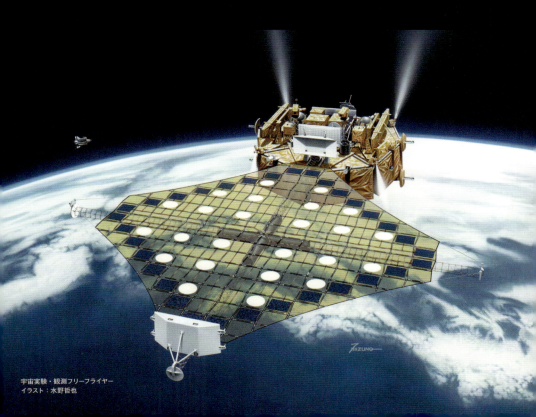

宇宙実験・観測フリーフライヤー
イラスト：水野哲也

身近なところでは、プシュッと缶のフタを開けると、缶の表面に凹凸のダイヤカットの形状が現れるキリンの缶チューハイ「氷結®」の仕組みも、ミウラ折りの応用です。

その他にも、エアバッグの折りたたみ方法や、簡単につぶせるペットボトル、軽くて強い車体や家具にも折り紙技術は応用されていると言われています。

Closer to home, the Miura Fold is used in the Kirin branded *'Hyoketsu'* drink cans, which reveal a diamond pattern when opened.
Nowadays, car airbags, easy-squash plastic bottles, light yet strong car bodies and even some furniture incorporate techniques from origami.

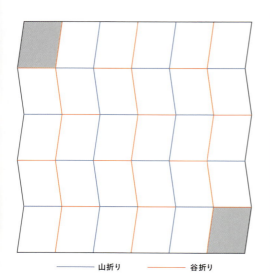

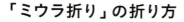

山折り　　谷折り

「ミウラ折り」の折り方

赤いユニコーン (2010)

黄色いカミキリムシ(2013)

サソリver.3(2008)

幸福の鳥(2011)

アリ・トリコロール(2013)

世界中へと広がっていった折り紙文化。今や、遊びやアートという枠組みを超え、その技法や仕組みは、宇宙、ファッション、医療、運輸、建築まで、幅広い分野で活用されつつあり、新たなイノベーションの鍵を握っていると言っても過言ではないのです。
日本が世界に誇る折り紙が、世界を変えていくのかもしれません。

The art of folding paper has progressed far beyond entertainment and beauty, and is now used in space, fashion, medical, transportation, architecture, and a variety of other fields. You could say that it provides a key to endless innovation.
The Japanese art of origami has the potential to change the world.

ゴッホとベアトリーチェ(2013)

寿司

TREASURE ⑤

Su**s**hi

Sushi is the ultimate culinary masterpiece,
combining beauty, passion, delicacy and grace.

日本を代表する料理「寿司」は、美しさ、情熱、繊細さ、優雅さ、すべてが詰まった人類の最高傑作です。

5

2013年にユネスコ無形文化遺産に認定されたことで、「和食」が世界中で注目されています。その中でも「寿司」は、日本の代表的な料理として、またヘルシーな健康食として世界中で知られています。海外でも「SUSHI」というそのままの名前で知られており、「SUSHIは人類の最高傑作」「職人の握るSUSHIは芸術品だ」とまで言う人がいるほど、世界中で愛されている料理なのです。

Since *washoku* (Japanese cuisine) was recognized as an intangible cultural heritage by UNESCO in 2013, Japanese cuisine has garnered ever more attention around the world. The most popular of all Japanese cuisine must be sushi.
The word sushi has now become synonymous with Japanese food, and some people go so far as to call it 'the greatest masterpiece of humankind,' and sushi made by master chefs is a true 'art.'

寿司職人の世界では「シャリ炊き3年、あわせ5年、握り一生」という言葉があり、一人前になるのに最低10年かかると言われています。長期にわたる修業を重ねた職人が、新鮮な魚介類を買い付け、丁寧に下ごしらえをして、徹底したこだわりと技術で握る寿司。カウンターの向こうで握る姿や立ち振る舞いも美しく、それはもはやただの食事ではありません。芸術的な美しさ、情熱、繊細さ、優雅さ、すべてが詰まっているのです。

There is a saying among sushi chefs that it takes 3 years to master cooking the rice, 5 years to master mixing the vinegar, and a lifetime to master shaping the rice base. It takes a minimum of 10 years before you can be recognized as a decent sushi chef. Through years of training, sushi chefs learn to choose the best cuts of fresh seafood, prepare it diligently and make the sushi with meticulous technique and dedication. The sight of a master sushi chef preparing sushi behind the counter is nothing short of beautiful, and the experience is not just a meal but an experience of artistic beauty, passion, delicacy and grace.

寿司には、魚を見極める知識や目、鮮度を生かす技術など、寿司職人のこだわりが詰め込まれています。

ただ魚（ネタ）が新鮮であれば良いわけではありません。その魚が最もおいしく食べられるようにたくさんの工夫がされているのです。魚の種類や状態に応じて、温度管理をしたり、いったん時間を置いたり、酢や塩でしめて旨味を最大限に引き出したり……最高の素材を最高の寿司として出すための丁寧な仕込みが、本当のおいしさを引き出しているのです。

The art of sushi requires a deep knowledge and skills garnered through years of training. A sense and eye for choosing the best cuts of fish, skills to make the most of fresh ingredients, and a host of other qualities are prerequisite for good sushi.

It's not just about the freshness of the fish. A number of things must be taken into account in order to maximize the flavor of the fish. Each type of fish has its own needs from temperature control, time before eating, use of vinegar or salt to bring out the best flavors, and more. To make the best sushi from the best ingredients requires diligent preparation and years of experience.

寿司のための飯（シャリ）の「握り方」は、寿司職人の技術が最も発揮されるところであり、様々な技があると言われています。
特別にブレンドしたお米や酢を使って作られるシャリは、季節や天気によって配合や炊き加減を変えたりもします。また赤身の魚には16g、白身の魚には18gのシャリといったように、ネタの種類によってシャリの量や密度も調整していたりもします。しかも熟練の職人は手の感覚だけでお米の量を調整できるのです。

職人が握ったシャリは、外側だけがしっかりしていて、中には空間があります。
空気を包むように絶妙の具合で握られているので、箸で持ち上げても壊れないのに、口の中に入れた途端にほどけるようにパッと広がるのです。最高峰の職人にもなると、米粒の外側3列だけを固めるという、信じられないような技を持っていると言われています。

Making the rice base, known as '*shari*,' is possibly the most difficult technique to master.
The combination of rice varieties and vinegar used to make sushi rice is adapted for the seasons and weather. 16g of rice is used for dark fish, 18g for light fish, and the size and density are adapted for each topping. Experienced sushi chefs make all these minute adjustments on the spot relying solely on the sensitivity of their own two hands.

The rice base of sushi made by sushi chefs has a firm exterior and soft interior. It is strong enough to be picked up by chopsticks but melts the moment you put it in your mouth. Some say the best sushi chefs hold the rice bases together with just the outer three layers of rice grains!

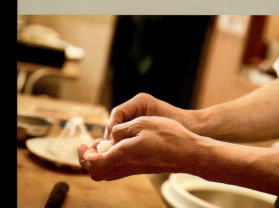

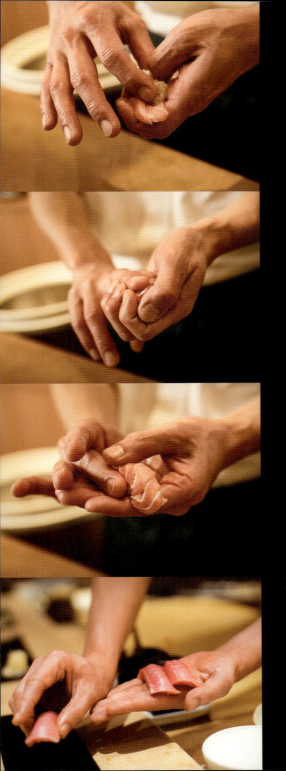

近年では、ロボットの握る寿司も品質が向上し、1皿100円で食べられる回転寿司も増え、誰でも気軽に寿司を楽しめるようになりました。しかし、本物の職人が握る寿司はまったくの別次元です。米本来のおいしさを引き出すために追求されたシャリ、丁寧に仕込んだ新鮮なネタ、そして食べた瞬間にふわっとほどける握りの技術、食べる人に合わせてシャリのサイズを調整するおもてなしの心……とてつもない時間と手間、技術、こだわりが詰まった本物の寿司こそ、世界に誇る寿司なのです。

In recent years, advances in technology have enabled robots to make sushi to a high standard, and some restaurants serve sushi for just 100 yen a plate. However, it should be known that these dishes simply do not compare to sushi made by master sushi chefs. The rice base is adapted to bring out the intrinsic flavors of rice, and the topping is prepared diligently to maximize the qualities of each type of fish or seafood. The texture of rice as you put the sushi in your mouth, and the thought that goes into altering the size for each customer... Years are spent refining the techniques necessary to produce top-quality sushi, and it is this creation that Japan proudly boasts to the world.

温

泉

日本が世界に誇る観光資源「ONSEN」は、
体と心を温め、疲れやストレスを和らげ、深い安らぎ、
解放感を味わう特別な場所です。

TREASURE ❻

ONSEN

HOT SPRING / SPA

Japanese have a special place in their heart for *onsen*,
natural thermal pools found all over the archipelago
where they go to warm their bodies and souls,
relieve physical and mental stress, and enjoy the sense of freedom.

6

火山が多い日本は、豊かな高温泉に恵まれており、源泉数は2万7,000本、全体の湧出量は毎分約260万リットルを超え、年間延べ利用人数は1億3,000万人にのぼる温泉大国です。

温泉旅館をはじめとし、銭湯、健康ランド、スパ、湯治場なども含めれば、温泉と呼ばれるものの数は世界一で、「日本人ほど温泉好きな国民はいない」と言われているほどです。狭い国土にもかかわらず、国中に温泉があり、その泉質も多種多様。日本の温泉の豊かさは、間違いなく世界に誇れるものなのです。

As a volcanic country, Japan is dotted with geothermally heated springs. There are around 27,000 known thermal springs around the country, from which a total of 2.6 million liters of hot water flow each minute. Each year, a total of 130 million people in Japan enjoy this refreshing pastime.

With public baths in many cities, health resorts, spas, hot spring resorts and many traditional inns offering their own private hot springs, the number of *onsen* facilities in Japan far exceeds any other country. *Onsen* are a part of the Japanese psyche. While *onsen* are ubiquitous around the small country, the water properties vary vastly from place to place, giving birth to a rich *onsen* culture.

日本人はお風呂が大好きです。他の国では、お風呂は「汚れを取って、身体を清潔にすること」ができれば十分と考えられ、シャワーだけで済ませることが多いですが、日本人は浴槽でお湯に浸かって、一日の疲れをゆっくり取る場所だと考えています。汚れた体のままで布団に入りたくない、夜ぐっすり眠りたい、ということで、お風呂は寝る前に入るのが一般的ですが、これも日本独自の習慣なのです。

Japanese people love their baths. In many countries, bathing is simply a matter of scrubbing the body clean. A shower does the job, and many people don't bother with the bathtub. For most Japanese, however, relaxing in a hot bathtub is an ideal way to relieve stress and unwind after a long day.
Generally, Japanese prefer to bathe in the evening, aiding better sleep and keeping their futon clean.

高温の水に「湯」という言葉があるのも、実は日本独自の表現です。他の国では「熱い水」としか言いません。英語で温泉はホットスプリングと言いますが、それは文字通り熱い水のことです。もちろん世界中に温泉はあります。しかし、他の国では温泉はアウトドアやレジャーとして楽しまれています。温泉というものは入って楽しむもので、温泉に入ることを「スイム」という言葉で表現したりします。
日本人にとって温泉は「浸かる」もの。体と心を温め、疲れやストレスを和らげ、深い安らぎ、解放感を味わう特別な場所なのです。

In Japan, there is a special word for 'hot water'. While regular water is *'mizu,'* hot water is called *'yu,'* or more commonly the honorific *'o-yu.'*
While natural hot springs occur in many countries, they are usually considered a place to play or swim. In Japan, however, people go to *onsen* to 'soak.' *Onsen* are a place to relax, warm the body and soul, relieve stress and find freedom of body and mind.

現存する温泉宿の中で最も長い歴史を持っているのは、山梨県にある「慶雲館」です。慶雲2年(705年)創業で、その歴史はなんと1300年以上。「現存する世界最古の宿」として、ギネス世界記録で認定を受けています。

The oldest hot spring inn in Japan is Keiunkan. Located in Yamanashi Prefecture, it was founded in the year 705 and has been in operation for over 1,300 years. Keiunkan is also recognized by Guinness as the oldest hotel in the world.

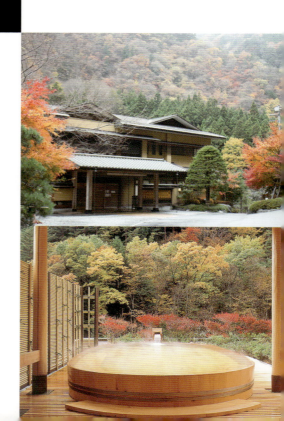

The Odaiba Onsen Monogatari, located in the Odaiba area of Tokyo, is one of the largest *onsen* facilities in Japan, and is designed to replicate scenes from the Edo Period. Water for the main bath is pumped up from 1,400 meters deep, and there are 13 different pools and areas including open air pools and saunas. It is a popular spot for foreign tourists to conveniently experience traditional Japanese *onsen* firsthand. The Odaiba *onsen* is ranked number 5 of the 20 coolest things for foreigners to do in Japan by Internet site *tripadvisor*.

東京・お台場にある「大江戸温泉物語」は、江戸の町並み、風情を再現した日本最大級の温泉施設です。地下1,400mから汲み上げた天然温泉をはじめ開放的な露天風呂やサウナなど13種類の多彩なお風呂があり、日本の伝統文化を手軽に体感できるということで、外国人観光客に大人気の施設となっています。
世界最大の旅行口コミサイト・トリップアドバイザーの「外国人がクールだと評価した日本の観光スポット20」では第5位にランクインしました。

他国とはまったく違う日本独自の温泉文化は、世界的に注目を集めています。温泉を目的に日本に旅行に来る観光客も年々増えており、「ONSEN」という言葉で世界中に広まりつつあります。「温泉」は世界に誇るべき日本の文化なのです。

The unique *onsen* culture of Japan is not seen anywhere else in the world, and is a major drawcard for more and more foreign tourists each year. Japanese hot springs have become so popular, the term '*onsen*' is starting to spread around the world.

Information

【慶雲館】
世界最古の宿、日本随一の湧出量の秘湯で至福のひとときを。

山梨県南巨摩郡早川町西山温泉 慶雲館

公式サイト https://www.keiunkan.co.jp/

【東京お台場 大江戸温泉物語】
日本最大級の元祖温泉テーマパークで、江戸の町にタイムスリップしよう。

東京都江東区青海2-6-3
ゆりかもめ線「テレコムセンター駅」より徒歩2分

公式サイト https://daiba.ooedoonsen.jp/

【Keiunkan Inn】
The oldest hotel in the world also offers one of the best onsen in Japan, making it an ideal place to experience traditional Japan.

Location: Nishiyama-Onsen, Hayakawa-cho, Minamikoma-gun, Yamanashi Prefecture

Official website https://www.keiunkan.co.jp/

【Oedo Onsen Monogatari hot spring complex】
One of the largest onsen complexes in Japan offers a time slip back to the Edo Period.

Location: 2-6-3 Aomi, Koto-ku, Tokyo
2 minutes on foot from Telecom Center Station on the Yurikamome Line

Official website https://daiba.ooedoonsen.jp/

生きる小宇宙、壮大な自然が凝縮された芸術「盆栽」。
700年前から続く日本の伝統芸術は、今、世界中でブームになっています。

TREASURE 7

BONSAI
The Art of Miniature Trees and Shrubs

Bonsai are a 'living miniature universe',
offering a glimpse of the majesty of nature within a small pot.
This 700-year old Japanese tradition is catching on fast around the world.

114 NEO ZIPANG

真柏　古渡烏泥長方　70cm
Juniperus chinensis var. Sargentii

盆栽とは、「盆（鉢）」と「栽（植物）」
が一体となり、壮大な自然が凝縮さ
れた芸術です。ハサミと針金を使い、
小さな鉢の中に描くように作られる作
品は、絵や彫刻とは違い、美しい季
節の移り変わりや生命の鼓動、雄大
な時の流れを感じることができます。
ただ植物自体を鑑賞する鉢植えと
は違い、自然美と人工美を調和させ
て、鉢の中に大自然を映し出す盆栽
は、生きる命の尊厳があり、奥深さ
があるのです。

The term *bonsai* is comprised of two
kanji characters. "盆" (*bon*) is a tray,
and "栽" (*sai*) is a plant. Together,
bonsai refers to the art of training
plants to create miniature versions of
nature in a tray or small pot using small
shears and wire. Unlike other forms of
art such as paintings and sculptures,
bonsai reflect the beauty of nature as it
changes through the seasons and
grows through the years, allowing you
to enjoy the rhythm of life and passing
of time. *Bonsai* have an aesthetic
beauty that sets them apart from
regular pot plants. They represent the
gigantic scale of nature and offer a
special insight into the meaning of life.

植物の年齢や、根の張り方から、幹の立ち上がり方、枝のつき方といった形が、盆栽の大きな評価ポイントになります。また、数百年と生き続ける盆栽は、骨董品と同じように「どんな人が持ち主だったか」もポイントになります。歴史上の有名な人物が持っていた盆栽などには箔がつくのです。中には、樹齢600年を超え、1億円の値がつくものもあります。

Size is not the only point for evaluating *bonsai*. Great importance is placed on age, roots, trunk shape and branch placement.
As with other antiques that last hundreds of years, it is important to know the history behind the *bonsai*. *Bonsai* previously owned by historically important people have added value. Some *bonsai* are over 600 years old and can fetch a price of 100 million yen.

約1300年前に中国で生まれ、約700年前の室町時代に日本へと伝わり、独自の進化を続けてきた「盆栽」。今では、英語、スペイン語、ドイツ語など様々な言語の辞書に「BONSAI」として訳されるほど浸透しており、世界中から「素晴らしい日本の伝統芸術」として高い評価を得ています。アメリカ、スペイン、フランスでは盆栽専門誌があり、さらにイタリアでは、専門学校や美術館まであるほどです。

The art of *bonsai* originated in China 1,300 years ago and has developed in a unique way since introduction to Japan during the Muromachi Period around 700 years ago.
Bonsai have become so widely recognized around the world that the word has made its way into dictionaries in English, Spanish and German. There are *bonsai* magazines in the USA, Spain and France, and even colleges with bonsai courses and a *bonsai* museum in Italy.

世界的な盆栽ブームの中、最先端な若者たちが「BONSAI」に夢中になり、新たな文化も生まれつつあります。バーやクラブなど人が集まる場所で、DJやバンドと競演しながら、ライブで作品を生み出す「盆栽パフォーマンス」が話題になったり、盆栽+AI技術で、「人間とコミュニケーションがとれる盆栽」というコンセプトで開発が進められていたりするのです。

As the popularity of *bonsai* spreads, new ways of enjoying this art are being developed by the next generation of *bonsai* lovers.
'*Bonsai* performances' at bars and clubs feature bonsai artists trimming *bonsai* on stage to music from DJs or live bands. Others are developing AI they hope will enable 'communication' with *bonsai*.

1989年に日本でスタートした世界中の盆栽好きが集まる「世界盆栽・水石大会」は、世界中で4年ごとに開催されています。アメリカ、韓国、ドイツ、プエルトリコ、中国で開かれてきたこの大会は、2017年に第8回大会として日本(埼玉)で開催されました。盆栽の故郷・日本での開催ということもあり、世界中から1,200人以上の愛好家が集い、約12万人が来場しました。そのうちの約8割を外国人が占めていたほど、盆栽は、国境を超えて親しまれているのです。

Since 1989 the World Bonsai Convention has been held every four years, attended by bonsai-lovers from around the world. After being held in the USA, Korea, Germany, Puerto Rico and China, the eighth convention was in Saitama, Japan in 2017. Its return to Japan, the home of bonsai, attracted over 1,200 specialists from around the world. Of the 120,000 people who attended the convention, around 80% were non-Japanese, illustrating just how popular bonsai have become around the world.

Information

【春花園BONSAI美術館】

日本三大賞である内閣総理大臣賞や東久邇宮文化褒賞を受賞した盆栽作家・小林國雄氏の「盆栽を世界により深く広めていきたい」という思いから誕生した盆栽の聖地。盆栽の魅力に触れる体験教室（有料：英語・中国語に対応）も実施しています。

東京都江戸川区新堀1-29-16
JR総武線「小岩駅」南口より京成バス（76番）で15分、「京葉口」より徒歩3分

公式サイト http://kunio-kobayashi.com/

【Shunkaen Bonsai Museum】

Established by bonsai master Kunio Kobayashi, recipient of the Prime Minister's Award and Higashi-Kuninomiya Culture Prize, two of the most coveted awards in Japan. The museum is a center for Kobayashi to promote bonsai to the world. Experience the joys of bonsai firsthand through workshops available in English and Chinese.

Location: 1-29-16 Nihori, Edogawa-Ku, Tokyo
15 minutes by Keisei Bus route 76 from the south exit of Koiwa Station on the JR Sobu Line. Get off at 'Keio-Guchi' stop, walk 3 minutes.

Official website http://kunio-kobayashi.com/

木造建築技術

1400年以上の時を超え、世界最古の木造建築が現存する日本。耐久性が高く、驚くほど精巧な木造建築の技術は、今もなお、伝統を受け継ぎながら最新を生み出し、世界を驚かせています。

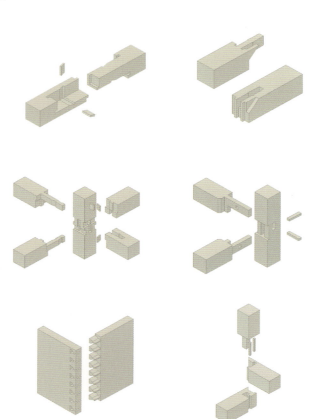

TREASURE ⑧

WOODEN BUILDINGS

At over 1,400 years, Japan is home to the world's oldest wooden building. The astounding durability and elaborate woodworking techniques passed down through the generations are still surprising the world with innovation rooted in history.

1400年以上の時を超え、世界最古の木造建築が今も残っている日本。地震や台風といった自然の脅威に常にさらされているこの国で、古い時代に建てられたたくさんの木造建築が倒壊せずに残っているという事実は、世界中を驚かせています。

Japan is home to the world's oldest wooden building. The fact that numerous wooden buildings have survived for centuries through earthquakes, typhoons and other natural disasters is testament to the world-class quality of Japanese wood craftsmanship.

「二重水組み継ぎ」
Niju-mizu-kumi-tsugi

「菊の逆組み継ぎ」
Kiku-no-gyaku-kumi-tsugi

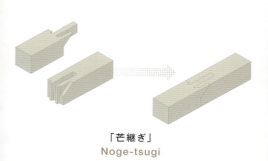

「芒継ぎ」
Noge-tsugi

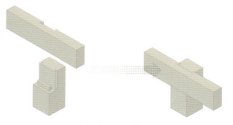

「吸付き差し仕口」
Suitsuki-sashi-shikuchi

世界有数の森林国である日本では、木材が豊富だったため、木造建築が主流となりました。また、夏には高温多湿になる風土なので、断熱性・吸湿性に優れていて、温度や湿度によって柔軟に状態を変える木は日本にはうってつけの材料だったのです。

The forest nation of Japan provided materials to develop sophisticated wooden architecture over the millennia. Wood is naturally suited to the Japanese climate, with good insulation properties, and an ability to absorb moisture during the hot, humid summer months.

地震大国である日本は、何度も地震を経験しながら、揺れを吸収する仕組みなどの耐震技術が進化してきました。大震災後、マグニチュード7以上の揺れでも倒壊することのなかった木造建築が注目され、その技術の高さが世界から注目されています。

Japan is extremely susceptible to earthquakes. Techniques to absorb and reduce the stresses on wooden buildings have been developed over the years, and many wooden buildings are known to have survived magnitude 7 earthquakes, drawing global attention.

「箱車知栓継ぎ」
Hako-shachisen-tsugi

「竿車知継ぎ」
Sao-shachi-tsugi

Japanese woodworkers have amazing joinery skills to create robust and durable buildings.
Wood is joined by intricate cuts, without the use of screws or nails, creating extremely strong joints that even the latest computer analysis cannot fully explain. There are around 200 different ways to fit the pieces of wood together utilizing the characteristics of wood and natural bends, requiring accurate and skillful joinery.
Twitter account 'The Joinery' (@TheJoinery_jp), featuring GIF animations illustrating accurate and beautiful joinery techniques, has become popular overseas.

日本の職人は、耐久性が高く、驚くほど精巧な木造建築技術を持っています。結合部分にネジや釘を使わず、木と木をはめ込むだけで固定して高い強度を生み出す木組みの技術は、現代のコンピューター解析を用いても解明できないほどだと言われています。木の性質や曲がりを見た上で一本一本を正確に切断し、木材同士をパズルのようにぴったりはめ込む組み合わせ方は、なんと200種類も存在するそうです。
精密で美しい奇跡のような木組みの技術を、GIFアニメを使って紹介しているTwitterアカウント・The Joinery (@TheJoinery_jp)が、海外でも大きな話題になっています。

TREASURE:8

現存している世界最古の木造建築は、約1400年前に建立されたと言われる法隆寺です。金堂や五重塔などの建造物11棟が、世界遺産に登録され、日本の国宝にも指定されています。特に、高さ31.5mの五重塔は、日本の建築の代表として知られていて、世界一美しい建造物とも言われています。その建築美もさることながら、1400年もの間その姿を保ち続けていることが非常に貴重なことであり、日本の木造建築技術の素晴らしさを証明してくれています。

The oldest surviving wooden buildings in Horyuji Temple complex in Nara are said to have been built 1,400 years ago. 11 buildings, including the main hall and five-story pagoda, are designated as World Heritage Sites, and house numerous National Treasures. At 31.5m tall, the five-story pagoda is one of the best-known examples of Japanese wooden carpentry, and is said by some to be the most beautiful building in the world. Aside from its aesthetic beauty, the fact that it has survived intact for 1,400 years is a miracle in itself, and testament to Japanese wooden construction methods.

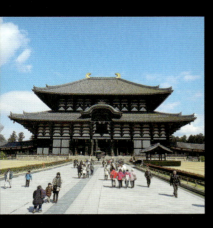

古い木造建築は、建築当初の状態から幾度となく解体修理が施され、今の時代に残っています。
これは日本独自の方法で、一度すべてを解体し、その中からまだ使える部材を残し、使えなくなった部材を新しいものに交換したり修繕したりしながら、組み直すのです。土壁も一度落としてから、新しい土と混ぜて作り直したりするので、膨大な手間と時間がかかります。ここにも日本人ならではの美学があるのです。

Old wooden buildings have been preserved to the modern age by a process of dismantling and repairing. In this method unique to Japan, the building is often completely dismantled and only the parts that need to be repaired are fixed or replaced. The building is then reassembled to its original state. Earthen walls are also repaired by breaking them down, mixing them with new clay, and rebuilding them in a process that is both labor and time intensive. This is yet another reflection of traditional Japanese aesthetics.

世の中には、最新の科学技術やテクノロジーが溢れていますが、日本建築は今もこの木造建築の伝統を受け継いでいます。例えば、高さ634mのタワー「東京スカイツリー」は、最新の制振技術「心柱制振」が採用されていますが、これは、法隆寺の五重塔と同じ「心柱」の構造によって支えられているのです。スカイツリーの中心部には長い柱が入っているのですが、これはタワーとは直接繋がっていない独立したものになっており、地震がきても、真ん中の柱とタワーの揺れにズレが生まれ、うち消し合うという原理なのです。

日本が誇る伝統を受け継ぎながら、最新技術を組み合わせることで、世界一のタワーが実現したのです。

While there is an abundance of modern science and technology around the world, Japanese architecture preserves ancient wooden building technology to this day.

Take, for example, the 634m high Tokyo Skytree completed in 2012. Tokyo Skytree features the latest seismic proofing technology which is modeled on the central pillar of Horyuji's five-story pagoda. This pillar is separate from the main tower structure, and moves separately in an earthquake, dampening the effect.

In this way, great Japanese traditions have been incorporated into the latest technology to create the world's tallest tower.

Information

【法隆寺】

現存する世界最古の木造建築物群。聖徳太子により奈良・斑鳩に建立された寺院。

奈良県生駒郡斑鳩町法隆寺山内1-1
公式サイト　http://www.horyuji.or.jp/

【東大寺大仏殿】

世界最大級の木造建築物（木造軸組構造で世界最大容積の建物）。
盧舎那仏坐像（奈良の大仏）が安置されている。

奈良県奈良市雑司町406−1 大仏殿
公式サイト　http://www.todaiji.or.jp/

【東京スカイツリー】

法隆寺五重塔と同じ制振構造を受け継いだ、高さ634m、世界一高いタワー。

東京都墨田区押上1-1-2
公式サイト　http://www.tokyo-skytree.jp/

【The Joinery (@TheJoinery_jp)】

伝統の「木組み」技術を、GIFアニメを使って紹介しているTwitterアカウント。
https://twitter.com/TheJoinery_jp

【Horyuji】

The oldest standing wooden building complex in the world. Built in Nara Prefecture by Prince Shotoku.

Location: 1-1 Horyuji Sannai, Ikaruga-cho, Ikoma-gun, Nara Prefecture

Official Website　http://www.horyuji.or.jp

【Great Buddha Hall at Todaiji Temple】

Housing the Great Statue of Buddha, the Great Buddha Hall is one of the largest wooden buildings in the world, and the largest in volume with complete wooden framework.

Location: Daibutsuden, 406-1 Zoushi-cho, Nara-shi, Nara Prefecture

Official Website　http://www.todaiji.or.jp/

【Tokyo Skytree】

At 634m, the highest tower in the world, it incorporates the same earthquake-dampening pillar structure as Horyuji's five-story pagoda

Location: 1-1-2 Oshiage, Sumida-Ku, Tokyo

**Official Website
http://www.tokyo-skytree.jp/**

【The Joinery (@TheJoinery_jp)】

Twitter account featuring GIF animations of traditional wood joining techniques

https://twitter.com/TheJoinery_jp

TREASURE ⑨

マンガ・アニメ
MANGA & ANIME

Japanese manga and anime are a rich artform with wide diversity covering a variety of genres. The unique perspectives offered in these art forms have captured the imaginations of children and adults alike around the world. They have evolved from mere entertainment to having a broad impact on society at large.

ジャンルが広く、バリエーションが豊かな日本のマンガとアニメ。その独特な世界観が、世界中の子ども、そして大人を魅了しています。今や、ただの娯楽という枠を超え、社会全体に影響を及ぼしています。

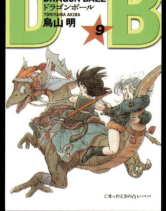

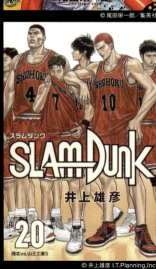

今や世界中にファンがいるジャパニーズポップカルチャー。その中核をなすのがマンガとアニメです。
クオリティが高く、ジャンルが幅広く、ストーリー性やメッセージ性が深い日本の作品は、たくさんの言語に翻訳され、世界中の人々に愛されています。

Japanese pop culture based on manga and anime has garnered a huge following around the world.
Japanese manga cover a wide variety of genres and are renowned for high quality art with intricate stories and deep messages. Japanese manga and anime have been translated into many languages and are now loved by people around the world.

©尾田栄一郎／集英社

伝説の超サイヤ人
©バードスタジオ／集英社

尾田栄一郎氏のマンガ『ONE PIECE』は42以上の国と地域で販売されており、全世界累計発行部数は4億5000万部を突破しています（2019年時点）。2015年には「最も多く発行された単一作家によるコミックシリーズ」としてギネス世界記録に認定されています。
鳥山明氏のマンガ『ドラゴンボール』は、40ヵ国以上で発売され、アニメは世界80以上の国と地域で放送されています。2013年には「世界で最もビデオゲーム化されたコミック」としてギネス世界記録に認定されています。

The manga 'ONE PIECE' written and illustrated by Eiichiro Oda is sold in over 42 countries and regions with global sales topping 450 million copies worldwide (as of 2019). In 2015 it was recognized by Guinness for 'the most copies published for the same comic book series by a single author'. 'Dragon Ball' created by Akira Toriyama is sold in over 40 countries and the anime is aired in over 80 countries and regions. In 2013 it was declared by Guinness as the most video game-ized comic in the world.

In most countries, manga and anime are considered the realm of children. In Japan, however, there are a huge range of manga and anime, some tailored to children like 'Doraemon', 'Precure' and 'Pocket Monsters', and others to teenagers and adults such as 'SLAM DUNK', 'ONE PIECE', 'Neon Genesis Evangelion' and Miyazaki classics such as 'My Neighbor Totoro'.

Topics cover a wide range of genres from sports, adventure, love, history, politics, cooking and economics, offering something for all age groups to enjoy.

海外では「マンガ」や「アニメ」は、子どもが楽しむものだとされています。しかし日本では、『ドラえもん』『プリキュア』『ポケットモンスター』といった子ども向けの作品から、『SLAM DUNK』『ONE PIECE』『新世紀エヴァンゲリオン』『となりのトトロ』など大人も楽しめる作品まで、バリエーションが非常に豊かです。

またスポーツ、冒険、恋愛から、歴史、政治、料理、経済まで、あらゆるジャンルで表現されており、老若男女を問わず幅広い年齢層が楽しめるのも大きな魅力です。

日本のマンガは独特な世界観を持っているため、英語の「COMIC」や「CARTOON」とは別のものとして認識されており、「マンガ（MANGA）」や「単行本（TANKOBON）」という言葉は、世界共通語としてあらゆる国で通じます。また日本のアニメも「ジャパニメーション」と呼ばれており、世界中でファンを獲得しています。

As Japanese manga have unique qualities that set them apart from English comics and cartoons, they are known by their Japanese names *manga* and *tankobon* around the world. Anime too are known as *Japanimation*, garnering a strong following around the world.

見て楽しむだけではなく、コスプレという新たな楽しみ方も、世界で大ブームを巻き起こしています。
コスプレとは「コスチュームプレー」を略した和製英語で、マンガやアニメのキャラクターに衣装やヘアスタイルなどを真似て、本物そっくりに扮装して楽しむことです。
2003年からは世界中の代表コスプレイヤーが集う「世界コスプレサミット(WCS)」が毎年開かれており、今や40以上の国や地域が参加するほどの盛り上がりを見せています。

Manga and anime are not just for watching. In recent years the *cosplay* boom has taken the world by storm. *Cosplay*, combining the words 'costume' and 'play', refers to the practice of dressing up to look like characters from manga and anime. Every year since 2003 people gather for the World Cosplay Summit which now attracts participants from over 40 countries and regions.

アニメで使用される楽曲「アニメソング」もアニソンと呼ばれ、世界中で熱い注目を集め、高い評価を獲得しています。2016年から始まった世界のアニソンファンに向けたイベント「Anisong World Matsuri」は年々盛り上がりを増しており、2018年にはアメリカ・ロサンゼルスで3日間開催で1万7,000人を動員、中国・上海では1万人を動員しました。

Songs and music used for anime are referred to as 'anisong' and have created a following of their own. The Anisong World Matsuri dedicated to fans of anisong has been gaining popularity since its inception in 2016. The three-day event in L.A in 2018 attracted 17,000 people, and the event in Shanghai brought together 10,000 anisong lovers.

Recently, more and more people have been making 'pilgrimages' to places associated with popular manga, such as featured locations, museums, or even the birthplace of anime and manga creators. This has been a big factor attracting overseas tourists to Japan. The backdrop to the global hit anime 'Your Name', which has been aired in over 125 countries and regions, was based on the rural Japanese town of Hida, in Gifu Prefecture. It has said that 'pilgrimages' to Hida have brought an estimated economic boost of nearly 20 billion yen.

Japanese manga and anime have crossed international borders and expanded past the realm of children's entertainment to have an effect on society at large.

アニメ・マンガなどの舞台となった場所や縁がある地に実際に訪れる「聖地巡礼」という文化も、新たに生まれています。外国人観光客が日本を訪れる目的のひとつに、この「聖地巡礼」が挙げられるほどです。

125以上の国や地域で爆発的ヒットとなったアニメ映画『君の名は。』の聖地である岐阜県の飛騨高山では、この聖地巡礼によって200億円近い経済効果をもたらされたとも言われています。

日本のマンガ・アニメは、国境を越え、そして、子どもたちの娯楽という枠を超えて、社会全体に影響を及ぼしているのです。

TREASURE ⑩

カプセルホテル

CAPSULE HOTELS

Taking minimalist lodgings to the extreme.
Not just cheap and easy, capsule hotels now cater to a wide range of needs,
offering unique experiences in Japan and abroad.

©9h nine hours Photo: Nacasa & Partners

日本発、世界に誇るミニマム宿泊施設「カプセルホテル」。「安くて寝るだけ」のスタイルだけではなく、多様なニーズに応え、様々な体験を提供する新たな文化とともに、世界へと広がっています。

TREASURE:10　137

宇宙船のような四角いカプセルがずらっと並ぶカプセルホテル。ひとつひとつのカプセルは、高さ・横幅1m、奥行き2mほどの大人ひとりが寝られる広さで、全体がベッドのようになっています。寝たままテレビが見られ、照明のスイッチにも手が届くように、機能的に配置された小さなホテルです。

一般的なカプセルホテルには、寝る場所だけではなく、パブリックスペースも充実しています。リラックスできる大浴場やサウナや水風呂、さらには、お風呂上がりにゆっくり過ごす休憩スペースやゲームコーナーなど、24時間ゆっくりと過ごせるように作られています。

Capsules are lined along the wall like some futuristic spaceship. Each one measuring 1m square by around 2m deep, there is barely enough room to lie down, but from this position you can enjoy watching TV and reach for the light switch easily.

Aside from individual sleeping capsules, most capsule hotels offer shared spaces where you can relax, enjoy a bath or sauna, or even play video games, all open 24-7 to enjoy at your leisure.

「安くて寝るだけ」というイメージで、サラリーマンたちが快適に手軽に低価格で泊まれる宿泊施設として国内で広まっていき、さらにアジアの大都市へと拡大していき、今や世界中あらゆる場所でカプセルホテルを見るようになりました。

WiseGuy Research Consultantsの調査によると、2016年に1億5,900万ドル（約179億円）だった世界のカプセルホテル市場が、2022年末には2億2,600万ドル（約254億円）に拡大すると予測されています。

実はこのカプセルホテル、日本発なのです。
カプセルホテルを設計したのは、建築家の黒川紀章氏。建築界のノーベル賞と言われるフランス建築アカデミーのゴールドメダルも受賞している日本が世界に誇る建築家です。
黒川紀章氏は1970年の大阪万博で、カプセルの中に各種の機能を盛り込んだ生活空間「住宅カプセル」を発表しました。カプセルを持ち運べば、設置場所がそのまま居住スペースになるという画期的なものでした。1972年には、そのカプセルを積み上げた建物「中銀カプセルタワービル」を東京・銀座に実際に誕生させました。
その後、そのカプセルにヒントを得たニュージャパン観光の社長が、黒川紀章氏に話を持ちかけ、「カプセル・イン大阪」という世界初のカプセルホテルを1979年に誕生させたのです。

While they began as a cheap option for businessmen who just wanted a bed to sleep in, capsule hotels have continued to expand their markets and can now be found in other large cities in Asia and around the world.

According to a 2016 survey by WiseGuy Research Consultants, the market for capsule hotels was 159 million dollars in 2016 and predicted to grow to 226 million dollars by the end of 2022.

Capsule hotels are the brainchild of renowned Japanese architect Kisho Kurokawa, recipient of the prestigious Gold Medal from the Académie d'Architecture, France.
Kurokawa first presented his concept at the 1970 Osaka Expo incorporating a range of features into a capsule. The revolutionary idea meant the capsule was actually mobile, allowing you to have a living space wherever you go. In 1972, the Nakagin Capsule Tower was built in the ritzy Ginza district of Tokyo, featuring stacks of capsule shaped apartments.
This caught the attention of director of New Japan Kanko who approached Kurokawa to establish the 'Capsule Inn Osaka'. The world's first capsule hotel was completed in 1979.

WALNUT　A02

世界初のカプセルホテルが誕生して約40年。最近では、「狭苦しくてチープな男性専用ホテル」といったネガティブイメージを覆す多様なカプセルホテルが次々と誕生しています。トップデザイナーがデザインする女性も利用しやすいスタイリッシュなものや、共用部分が充実していて、Wi-Fi完備のコワーキングスペースを併設するもの、IoTテクノロジーを導入し、カプセル内にいてもトイレや大浴場の混雑状況がわかるハイテクなものまで、あらゆるスタイルのカプセルホテルが登場しています。

©9h nine hours Photo: Nacasa & Partners
©9h nine hours Photo: Nacasa & Partners

©The Millennials Photo: DAISUKE SHIMA

©The Millennials Photo: DAISUKE SHIMA

©The Millennials Photo: DAISUKE SHIMA

©The Millennials Photo: DAISUKE SHIMA

©The Millennials Photo: DAISUKE SHIMA

©The Millennials Photo: DAISUKE SHIMA

Now, nearly 40 years since the first capsule hotel, new improvements are helping to shed the negative 'stingy-man' stigma that has been attached to the hotels. With the help of popular designers, stylish designs appealing to women, better shared facilities with Wi-Fi and co-working spaces and incorporation of IoT technology allowing customers to check availability of washrooms, baths, and other facilities from the comfort of their own capsule, these hotels are becoming even more popular with a wider audience.

TREASURE:10 **141**

日本が世界に誇るミニマム宿泊スタイル、カプセルホテル。一時は「ウサギ小屋」と揶揄されていたカプセルホテルは、時代とともに変化し、多様化するニーズを先取りし、新たな体験を提供するようになっています。きっと、未来の旅人たちの新たな選択肢となるようなカプセルホテルが、これから世界中に続々と誕生するに違いありません。

Once ridiculed as 'rabbit hutches,' capsule hotels have evolved with the times, accommodating ever changing needs of a wide range of customers, and offering new and unique experiences. I'm sure more and more innovative capsule hotels will continue to appear, catering to the needs of future travelers around the world.

©hotel zen tokyo

©hotel zen tokyo

©9h nine hours Photo: Nacasa & Partners

Information

【カプセル・イン大阪】（大阪）

世界初カプセルホテル。カプセルホテルの設計は「2100年のビジネスホテル」をコンセプトに、建築家の黒川紀章氏が担当。元祖「スリープカプセル」も現役で活躍しています。

大阪府大阪市北区堂山町9-5
公式サイト　http://www.umedasauna-newjapan.jp/capsule/

【The Millennials】（東京・京都・福岡）

「未来が見える宿泊体験」をテーマに、東京・渋谷や京都・河原町、福岡・博多に展開するライフスタイルホテル。IoT搭載ですべての機能をiPodで操作する客室のほか、ワークスペース、セルフキッチンなど充実した共用ラウンジを備えた未来型カプセルホテル。

公式サイト　https://www.themillennials.jp/

【9h nine hours（ナインアワーズ）】（仙台・東京・京都・大阪・福岡）

1h（汗を洗い流す）＋7h（眠る）＋1h（身支度）、計9時間の3つの基本行動に特化して、機能性とクオリティを徹底追求した、都市生活にフィットする宿泊機能と新しい滞在価値を提供する「ナインアワーズ」。

公式サイト https://ninehours.co.jp/

【hotel zen tokyo】（東京）

「禅」をテーマに「泊まれる茶室」をコンセプトにした茶室型カプセルホテル。かつて茶人たちが理想の茶室空間とした「市中の山居」を目指して、都会の喧騒の中に、まるで山奥のような異空間を設えています。

東京都中央区日本橋人形町1-5-8
公式サイト https://www.hotelzen.jp/

【Capsule Inn Osaka】 (Osaka)

The world's first capsule hotel designed by architect Kisho Kurokawa is still in operation with the concept 'Business Hotel for 2100'. You can still find the original 'sleep capsules' in use!

9-5 Doyama-cho, Kita-ku, Osaka City
Official Website
http://www.umedasauna-newjapan.jp/capsule/

【The Millennials】 (Tokyo, Kyoto, Fukuoka)

This futuristic hotel 'The Future of Lodging' with three locations in Tokyo's Shibuya ward, Kyoto's Kawaramachi and Fukuoka's Hakata offers not only lodging, but a new lifestyle. It offers a workspace, kitchen, communal lounge and has IoT that allows you to control all functions with an iPod.

Official Website
https://www.themillennials.jp/

【9h Nine Hours】

(Sendai, Tokyo, Kyoto, Osaka, Fukuoka)

This new urban hotel focuses on the time required to reset after a long day and prepare for the new day. One hour to wash, seven to sleep, and one more to get ready for the new day. Enjoy nine high quality hours with the best amenities offered at this new chain of specialist hotels.

Official Website https://ninehours.co.jp/

【hotel zen tokyo】 (Tokyo)

Teahouse inspired 'Zen' pods offer a taste of authentic Japan in modern Tokyo. True to the traditional ideal of creating nature within the room, Hotel Zen has succeeded in bringing a minimalist Zen-like tranquility into the heart of Tokyo.

1-5-8 Ningyocho, Nihonbashi, Chuo-ku, Tokyo
Official Website https://www.hotelzen.jp/

NEO CULTURE

伝統 × 最新

21世紀のネオカルチャーを紹介

Tradition × Innovation
An introduction to neo-culture in 21st-century Japan

そして、ここからは、
現代の日本ならではの新しい表現を見てみましょう。
古くから伝わる日本独自の伝統。
世界最先端の技術、最新のアートやエンターテイメント。
21世紀の日本には、伝統と最新をうまくミックスすることから生まれた、
素晴らしい表現が溢れています。
本当は、すべてを紹介したいくらいですが、
ここでは、僕らの感性で選んだ、とんがった新しい日本のカルチャーを
8つ紹介します。
ガイド情報も掲載しているので、気になるものがあったら、ぜひ、現場
に足を運んで、肌で感じてみてください。

From here we'll look at the new face of Japanese culture.
With a rich heritage of traditions unique to Japan coexisting alongside groundbreaking technology and the latest in art and entertainment, 21st-century Japan has found a way to create wonderful new forms of expression.
There are so many amazing things to introduce about modern Japan, it was a tough job to whittle them down to eight that caught our attention the most.
If you find something that grabs your attention, please use the information provided to go and experience these wonders for yourself.

日本画 × ガンダム

Ni Hon Ga

TRADITIONAL JAPANESE PAINTINGS × GUNDAM

Tenmyouya Hisashi is a Japanese artist who has put an exciting contemporary touch on traditional Japanese paintings. While staying true to traditional methods, he has created a new style that breaks free of accepted norms, creating unconventional and striking works of original art.

RX-78-2 Kabuki-mono 2005 Version 2000×2000mm 2005 ©Tenmyouya Hisashi ©創通エージェンシー・サンライズ

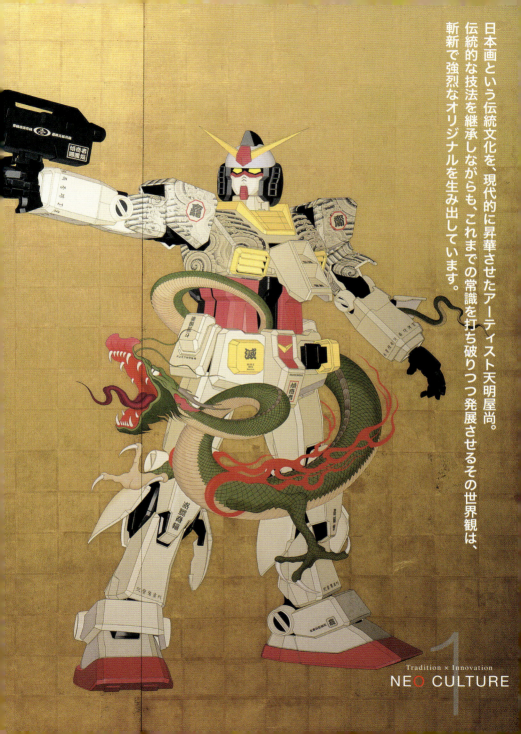

1870年代にヨーロッパからもたらされた油絵や水彩画などの洋画に対して、それまでの日本にあった伝統的な技法・形式・様式に従って岩絵具で描かれた絵画のことを「日本画」と言います。江戸時代の風俗をチラシやポスターなどで表した浮世絵や、花と鳥などを描いて四季の素晴らしさを表現した花鳥画など、日本画からはその時代時代の風俗や心情が見て取れます。

日本画の歴史の中には、「画聖」「画狂」「画鬼」と名乗っていた画家がいます。

'Nihonga' is a term for traditional Japanese paintings that had developed in Japan prior to the introduction of oil paintings from Europe in the 1870s. Abiding by a set of rules determining techniques, conventions and materials, Nihonga give us a glimpse into the customs and psyche of old Japan through ukiyoe featuring posters and leaflets, and kachoga showing flowers and birds of the seasons.

There are different terms attached to certain genius or master painters in history; 'Ga-sei', 'Ga-kyo' and 'Ga-ki'.

画聖は、室町時代に活躍した水墨画家・雪舟。
「水墨画を極めることは禅を極める」と、水墨画の本場である明(王朝)へ渡り、3年修業した雪舟は、個性豊かな水墨山水画様式を完成させ、後世に多大な影響を与えました。日本美術史上最多となる6点もの作品が国宝に指定されています。

'Ga-sei' (lit. painting saint') refers to Sesshuu, a prominent ink artist of the Muromachi Period.
Also a Zen monk, Sesshuu famously proclaimed, 'mastering ink painting is akin to mastering Zen.' He traveled to Ming China to study landscape painting, further developing the art on return to Japan, creating his own original style of ink and wash painting. A record six of his works are recognized as national treasures, more than any other artist in the history of Japan.

画狂は、世界一有名な日本の画家、江戸後期の浮世絵師・葛飾北斎。描いた作品は3万点を超え、ゴッホ、モネ、ルノワールなど絵画の巨匠たちにも大きな影響を与えたと言われています。
海外では「グレートウェーブ」と呼ばれる代表作「富嶽三十六景 神奈川沖浪裏」の大波の作品は、クリスティーズ・ニューヨークのオークションで、94万3,500ドル（約1億400万円）で売却され、1枚の日本版画としての世界新記録を樹立しました。

'Ga-kyo' (lit. 'painting lunatic') refers to Hokusai Katsushika, an *ukiyoe* master of the latter Edo Period and perhaps the most famous Japanese artist of all time.
During his time, he produced over 30,000 pictures which are said to have influenced such artistic greats as van Gogh, Monet and Renoir.
Hokusai's masterpieces include the iconic woodblock print 'The great wave off Kanagawa' which sold for a record $943,500 at Christie's Auction in New York, the highest price ever paid for a single Japanese print.

画鬼は、幕末から明治にかけて活躍した天才絵師・河鍋暁斎（かわなべきょうさい）。流派にとらわれない独創的な画法で、ユーモアを交えながら仏画や山水画から戯画、風刺画まで様々なジャンルの作品を生み出し、「日本画の表現領域を広げ続けた桁外れの絵師」との呼び声も高く、海外でも高く評価されています。政府の役人を風刺する絵を描いて捕らえられたこともある反骨精神溢れる人物で、画力だけではなく、その生き方も魅力と言われています。

河鍋暁斎「化々学校」／提供：アフロ

'Ga-ki' (lit. 'painting demon') refers to art virtuoso Kyosai Kawanabe who lived through the end of the Edo Period into the Meiji Period. His groundbreaking style was not constrained by any individual artistic style, but incorporated humor into Buddhist paintings and landscapes, caricatures and even satirical art. He was an extraordinary artist who is often credited with 'expanding the expressive realm of *Nihonga*' and is highly regarded around the world. He also had a well-known rebellious side, once being apprehended for painting satirical caricatures of political officials, making him famous not only for his art, but his attitude and lifestyle as well.

Archery 900×700mm 2008 ©Tenmyouya Hisashi

「画聖」雪舟、「画狂」葛飾北斎、「画鬼」河鍋暁斎に続くべく、自ら「画強」と名乗る現代美術作家がいます。その名も「天明屋尚」。

現代的なテーマを日本画的な手法を用いて描くそのスタイルは、「ネオ日本画」を標榜し、絵筆で闘う「武闘派」を名乗り、絵画、雑誌、新聞挿画、ポスター、映画美術など多様な形態で作品を発表しています。

Following in the footsteps of masters Sesshuu, Hokusai and Kyosai, contemporary artist Tenmyouya Hisashi is a self-proclaimed 'Ga-kyo,' or self-titled 'Painting Strength'
Using traditional Nihonga techniques to portray contemporary themes in his new 'neo-Nihonga' style which he executes as a 'militant fighting with brushes'. Hisashi's neo-Nihonga style is not restricted to painting, but is applied to magazine and newspaper illustrations, posters and movie art.

日本画という伝統文化を現代的に昇華させる天明屋尚氏の独創的なセンスは、世界的にも非常に高い評価を得ており、描いた作品がニューヨーク・タイムズの1面を飾ったこともあります。2006年サッカー W杯ドイツ大会のFIFAワールドカップ公式アートポスターでは、日本代表作家として唯一選出され、海外から見たステレオタイプな日本を象徴する戦国武将の鎧兜でサッカーの対戦が表現されています。

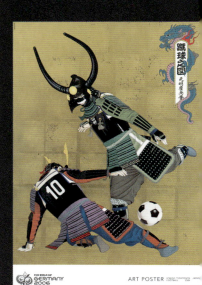

Football 882×662mm ©Hisashi Tenmyouya, ©2005 FIF

Tenmyouya Hisashi's unique artisti sense is widely credited with revivin traditional Japanese paintings as contemporary art, and his art has eve adorned the cover of the New Yor Times.
Hisashi was the only Japanese artis chosen for the 2006 FIFA soccer Worl Cup official art poster, depictin stereotypical Japanese feudal warlord in full regalia facing off at soccer.

150 NEO ZIPANG

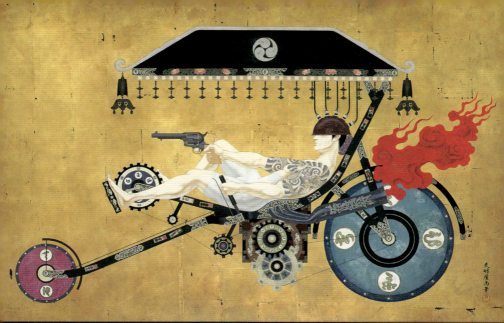
Japanese Spirit #1 1065×1585mm 1997 ©Tenmyouya Hisashi

Black Helmet in the Shape of a Cloaked Robot 1500×3000mm 2016 ©Tenmyouya Hisashi

Contemporary Japanese Youth Culture Scroll - "Para-para (Great Empire of Japan) vs. Break-dancing (America)" 598×420mm 2001 ©Tenmyouya Hisashi

Neo Thousand Armed Kannon 2273×1620mm 2002 ©Tenmyouya Hisashi

Kanji Irises Leaves Graffiti Cedar Panel Door Painting,
"Kill with a Single Blow, Special Attack Party"
1854×1770mm 2000 ©Tenmyouya Hisashi

RX-78-2 Kabuki-mono 2005 Version
2000×2000mm 2005 ©Tenmyouya Hisashi
© 創通エージェンシー・サンライズ

機関銃やナイフを千手観音のすべての手に持たせた、第6回岡本太郎記念現代芸術大賞優秀賞受賞作品「ネオ千手観音」。人力で駆動する空想のマシンに刺青の男が武装している「Japanese Spiritシリーズ」。100年前の杉戸に漢字でグラフィティを描いた「漢字具羅富異帝杉戸絵」。現代の事件を鋭い視点で切り取る「武闘派列伝　反骨諷刺絵巻シリーズ」など、奇想な画風、繊細で華麗な技、大胆で奇抜なアイデアで多くの作品群を発表しています。

His piece 'Neo Thousand Armed Kannon' depicting a heavily armed machine gun and knife-wielding deity won the 6th Taro Okamoto Award for Contemporary Art, while his series 'Japanese Spirit' depicts a tattooed man on an imaginary man-powered machine. 'Kanji Irises Leave Graffiti Cedar Panel Door Painting' is a 100-year-old cedar door with graffiti on it, while his series 'Illustrated Scroll of Defiant Satire, Legendary Warriors Series' consists of satirical images which take a rebellious poke at modern incidents. Each piece offers a new and fantastic approach on the subject matter, backed by refined and brilliant artistic skills.

天明屋尚氏のネオ日本画の中で特に注目を集めた作品は、日本を代表するロボットアニメ「機動戦士ガンダム」をモチーフにした「RX-78-2 傾奇者 2005 Version」。
2005年に開催された企画展「GUNDAM 来たるべき未来のために」のために制作したもので、刺青をしたガンダムとそれに絡みつく竜を、日本伝統絵画の金箔表現を用いて描いた作品です。
この作品は、香港のクリスティーズ・オークションで480万香港ドル（約6,300万円）で落札され、大きな話題となりました。

One of the most famous of Tenmyouya Hisashi's *neo-Nihonga* is his depiction of the famous Japanese robot Gundam, inked up and entwined in a dragon. Created for the 2005 GUNDAM exhibition, the piece 'RX-78-2 Kabuki-mono 2005 Version' featuring traditional gold leaf artwork was sold for an astounding 4.8 million Hong Kong Dollars at Christie's Auction in Hong Kong.

NEO CULTURE:1 153

日本画の伝統的な技法を継承しながらも、これまでの常識を打ち破りつつ発展させ、現代的なテーマを積極的に取り入れているネオ日本画の世界観は、唯一無二のもの。伝統から生まれる斬新で強烈なオリジナルこそが、NEO ZIPANGを生み出していくのです。

The *neo-Nihonga* movement serves to preserve traditional *Nihonga* techniques while developing them in innovative ways, readily adopting contemporary themes to create a new artistic expression like no other. This extravagant originality based on a twist of tradition is the driving force behind NEO ZIPANG.

Baku image 1880x1740mm 2010 ©Tenmyouya Hisashi

Rhyme 1270x3000mm 2012 ©Tenmyouya Hisashi

Information

【天明屋尚 オフィシャルサイト】 http://tenmyouya.com/
現代美術家「天明屋尚」のオフィシャルサイト

映画【≒天明屋尚 Near Equal Tenmyouya Hisashi】
天明屋尚の素顔に迫るドキュメンタリー映画。
監督: 石崎豪 / 販売元: ビー・ビー・ビー株式会社 / 時間: 98 分

【Tenmyouya Hisashi Official Website】 http://tenmyouya.com/
Official Website of contemporary artist Tenmyouya Hisashi

【≒Tenmyouya Hisashi 'Near Equal Tenmyouya Hisashi'】
A documentary on the man behind the name.
Director: Ishizaki Go / Distributor: B.B.B. Inc. / Running time: 98 minutes

花火
Ha Na Bi

×

最先端テクノロジー

FIREWORKS
CUTTING-EDGE TECHNOLOGY

A world-first entertainment show 'Star Island' realizes a perfect syncronisation of live performance, lighting and 3D sound with traditional Japanese fireworks, said to be the most beautiful in the world.
This next-generation pyrotechnic show stimulates all five senses, extending from Japan to the world, and into the future.

Tradition × Innovation
NEO CULTURE
2

世界で最も美しいと称される日本の伝統文化「花火」と最先端テクノロジー「3Dサウンド」「ライティング」「ショーパフォーマンス」が完全シンクロし、世界初のエンターテインメント「STAR ISLAND」が誕生。五感をフル活用して楽しめる 次世代型の花火文化を生み出し、日本から世界へ発信し、未来へと繋いでいます。

世界で最も美しいと称され、世界中に輸出されている日本の花火。火薬や花火の歴史は中国やヨーロッパの方が古いと言われていますが、花火に「美しさ」という芸術性を求め続け、成熟させてきた文化は日本独特のものです。海外の花火では迫力や激しい爆発音が求められますが、日本の花火はその先にある「奥深さ」と「美」を追求し続けているのです。その結果、日本の花火は世界一精巧で華やかだと言われるようになりました。日本の花火は、火薬を爆発させるただの化学反応ではなく、長年かけて磨き上げられた伝統芸術なのです。

Japanese fireworks, known for their exquisite beauty, are exported around the world. While China and Europe have a longer history of gunpowder and fireworks, it was in Japan that techniques were refined to create the beautiful and impressive pyrotechnic shows we know today.
While most firework shows around the world rely on size and sound, Japanese fireworks go further to seek artistic beauty and depth of feeling. This has led to Japanese fireworks being described as the most sophisticated and glamorous in the world. Through years of refinement, a tradition has developed that goes beyond the simple chemical reaction of setting off gunpowder.

海外の花火は、独立記念日や年末のカウントダウンといったお祝い事の際に、盛り上げるために打ち上げられるのが一般的です。つまり花火はお祝いの引き立て役なのです。しかし、日本の場合は「花火大会」として、花火自体がメインのイベントとして開催されます。お祝いのために何発か上げるものとは違い、打ち上げる玉数も多く、時間も長いのが大きな魅力です。しかもその花火大会は日本中でいろんな日に開催されているので、全国で多種多様な花火大会をいくつも見ることができるのです。

In many countries, fireworks are used for celebrations such as Independence Day or New Year's countdown. They are an accessory for a special event.
Japan, however, has events dedicated to enjoying the fireworks themselves. These events show off a huge number of fireworks over an extended time in what can easily be deemed as a pyrotechnical spectacular. These firework shows are held on different days throughout the country, so you can enjoy a wide variety of shows at different times and locations.

2017年、「美しさ」という芸術性を求め続けた日本の花火が、さらなる進化を遂げました。日本の伝統文化である花火が、「3Dサウンド」や「ライティング」などの最先端テクノロジーやパフォーマンスと完全シンクロし、大都会の摩天楼をバックに開催される新たな花火エンターテインメント「STAR ISLAND」が生まれたのです。

In 2017, the pursuit of beauty in Japanese fireworks took another leap forward. Traditional Japanese fireworks were perfectly synchronized with the latest 3D sound and lighting technology to create STAR ISLAND, a brand-new form of entertainment against a backdrop of skyscrapers.

The inaugural 2017 show and following 2018 show at Tokyo's Odaiba Kaihin Park took the unusual step of charging a fee for all viewing areas. The first ever international show in 2018, STAR ISLAND SINGAPORE COUNTDOWN EDITION backed by the Singapore government was the main attraction for the crowd of 500,000 who had gathered from around the world at Marina Bay in Singapore.

2017年に初開催し、2年連続で東京・お台場海浜公園で行われた公演は、花火イベントとしては異例の全席有料開催でチケットがすべて事前完売。2018年末には、初の海外進出を果たし、シンガポール政府後援のアジア最大級カウントダウンイベントのメインコンテンツとして採用され、「STAR ISLAND SINGAPORE COUNTDOWN EDITION」を開催、会場のマリーナベイに世界中から集まった約50万人を魅了しました。

「STAR ISLAND」は、地球上のどこにでも現れる可能性のある、現実とのパラレルワールドで、その土地の自然と文化・伝統を感じることができるロケーションエンターテインメントでもあります。会場の砂浜を埋め尽くす300台を超えるスピーカーによって創り出される3Dサウンドの立体的な音楽と世界最高峰のパフォーマンス、夜空に打ち上げられる花火が完全にシンクロした世界観はまさに圧巻。これまでの花火大会の概念を変え、花火エンターテインメントとして昇華しており、これまでにない新感覚を体感できます。

STAR ISLAND can be adapted to anywhere in the world. The so-called 'location entertainment' creates a parallel world expressing the nature, culture and traditions of each location. Over 300 speakers lining the beach produce 3D sound that engulfs the audience as a groundbreaking performance of fireworks light up the night sky in a perfectly synchronized collaboration that reveals a truly stunning view of our world. This 'pyrotechnic entertainment' totally exceeds the current concept of firework shows, offering a completely new experience.

150年以上の歴史を持つ老舗花火屋「丸玉屋小勝煙火店」をはじめ、「紅屋青木煙火店」「マルゴー」の花火職人が作る1万発を超える花火と、国内外で活躍するトップクリエイターがタッグを組み、花火、3Dサウンド、ライティング、パフォーマンスを完全シンクロさせ、新しい花火エンターテインメントが生み出されます。また"花火の観方を変える"べく、ベッドで寝ながら花火を楽しめる「ベッドエリア」や、食事をしながら楽しめる「ディナーエリア」、子どもと一緒に鑑賞できる「キッズエリア」等を設け、今までの花火鑑賞とは一線を画しています。
伝統文化と最先端テクノロジーの融合により、五感をフル活用して楽しめる新しい花火文化を生み出し、日本から世界へ発信し、未来へと繋いでいます。

The show features over 10,000 individual pyrotechnic rounds produced by experts from such renowned firework makers as Marugo, Beniya-Aoki, and Marutamaya Ogatsu Fireworks, which has a history of over 150 years. With the aid of a team of top creators, these world-class fireworks are seamlessly combined with 3D sound, lighting and live performances creating a new form of pyrotechnic entertainment. In an attempt to create new ways of enjoying fireworks, several areas such as a bed area, dinner area and kid's area are set up, allowing you to enjoy the show reclined, while eating, or playing with your kids.

Information

STAR ISLAND

未来型花火エンターテインメント
「STAR ISLAND」を体感しに行こう。

http://www.star-island.jp

STAR ISLAND

Experience the future of pyrotechnic entertainment with STAR ISLAND.

http://www.star-island.jp

日本の伝統文化「花火」を新たな形で演出し、無限の可能性を感じさせてくれる未来型花火エンターテインメント「STAR ISLAND」。日本が世界に誇るべき伝統を、昔ながらの形のままで継承するのではなく、今の時代の人々に合った形へアップデートさせて継承していくという、NEO ZIPANGスタイルのヒントが、ここには溢れています。

Futuristic pyrotechnic entertainment STAR ISLAND offers infinite potential to showcase traditional Japanese fireworks in a new way.
This collaboration of superb Japanese traditions updated for the modern times and passed on to the future offers more hints for the NEW ZIPANG style.

茶道
Sa Do

現代ライフスタイル

TEA CEREMONY × MODERN LIFESTYLE

'*Sado*' or Tea Ceremony is a well-known Japanese composite art. With respect for traditions, a new form of tea ceremony has emerged, taking on a new style with originality and ingenuity suited to the modern lifestyle. This '*neo sado*' has been gaining popularity in Japan and abroad.

Tradition × Innovation
NEO CULTURE
3

日本の総合芸術とも言われる茶道。その伝統を重んじながらも、現代のライフスタイルに合わせ、創意工夫を加えて独自のスタイルを生み出し続ける「新しい茶道」が、国内外で多くの共感を呼び、高い評価を得ています。

外国人旅行者に、日本で一度は体験してみたいことを聞くと、必ず日本の伝統文化である「TEA CEREMONY＝茶道」が挙がってきます。
茶道とは伝統的な様式に則ってお茶を振る舞う儀式のことで、茶の湯とも言います。それは、ただお茶を入れて飲むだけのことではなく、茶室や庭といった空間や、茶道具や茶室に飾る美術品、客人をおもてなしするための作法、そして生きる目的や考え方に至るまで、すべてが融合した総合芸術と言われています。

お茶はもともと中国から伝わってきました。書物で伝わったお茶を、禅僧が中国から輸入し、そこから徐々に儀式化されながら広がっていきました。その後、天下人・織田信長、豊臣秀吉の2人に仕えた"茶聖"千利休が、伝統儀式としての茶道の原型をつくり上げたのです。茶道という美を追い続けた千利休は、現代日本人の美的感覚やおもてなし精神の基礎を築いたと言っても過言ではありません。

When asked what they most want to experience in Japan, many foreign tourists will answer 'tea ceremony,' or '*sado*'.
Also known as '*chanoyu*,' the tea ceremony is a traditional way of entertaining guests with tea, following a strict set of protocols.
The tea ceremony is not simply about serving tea to a guest, but begins with the environment, such as a teahouse or garden, the implements used to prepare the tea, artwork decorating the walls, mannerisms to graciously receive the guests, and continues on to pondering the meaning of life, making it a truly composite art form.

The tea itself was originally brought from China. Learning about the tea from literature, Zen priests brought this tea to Japan where it was prepared with ever more ritualization, spreading throughout Japan. Later, tea master Sen no Rikyu who served under *daimyo* Nobunaga Oda and Hideyoshi Toyotomi, formalized the art form as we know it today, cementing its place as a traditional ceremony. One could say that modern day Japanese artistic sense and hospitality stems from the work of Sen no Rikyu in his pursuit of beauty through *sado*.

SHUHALLY

There is a contemporary master of tea ceremony who is breathing a new, contemporary life into the ancient tradition of *sado*. Souryou Matsumura heads the SHUHALLY Project, aiming to make the art of *chanoyu* freer and more fun. The name SHUHALLY originates from words Sen no Rikyu himself left, outlining the spirit of tea ceremony with three kanji; '*shu*' (protect), '*ha*' (break) and '*ri*' (separate). 'So long as you are trying to break tradition, you cannot help but protect it.' With this in mind, SHUHALLY aim to create a new form of *sado* while maintaining the spirit of tea masters through history.

SHUHALLY

日本古来の伝統文化である茶道に、現代の息吹を吹き込み、既成概念を塗り替えている茶道家がいます。茶の湯をもっと自由に、もっと愉しくすることを目指す「SHUHALLYプロジェクト」を主宰する松村宗亮氏です。
「SHUHALLY」の語源は千利休が残した茶道の心得「守・破・離」から。「伝統を破ろう破ろうと思っているうちは"守"を抜け出せない」という考えで、歴史を繋いできた茶人の想いを引き継ぎながら、まったく新しい茶道を表現しています。

千利休が残した茶道の伝統を重んじながらも、現代のライフスタイルに合わせ、創意工夫を加えて独自のスタイルを生み出し続けるSHUHALLYの活動は、国内外で共感を呼び、高い評価を得ています。

全国の百貨店やギャラリー、また海外（ベルギー、スペイン、アメリカ、フランス、ポーランド　スイス、香港、シンガポール、韓国等）や首相公邸から招かれるなど多数の茶会をプロデュース。コンテンポラリーアートや漫画、ヒューマンビートボックスといった様々なジャンルとのコラボレーションも積極的に行いながら、日本文化の新たな伝統の開拓・発信に努め幅広く活動を続けています。

While paying tribute to the traditions established by Sen no Rikyu, SHUHALLY have added an original twist, creating a new style for the modern lifestyle that has been well received and regarded highly in Japan and abroad.
They have gone on to hold numerous tea ceremonies at department stores and galleries in Japan and abroad (Belgium, Spain, the USA, France, Poland, Switzerland, Hong Kong, Singapore, Korea, and more) and have been summoned to the official residence of the prime minister of Japan. They pursue collaborations with contemporary art, manga, and even human beat-box artists, covering a wide range of genres in an attempt to expand and promote a new tradition within Japanese culture.

裏千家十六代家元・坐忘斎により命名され
たSHUHALLYのオリジナル茶室「文彩庵」
は、新しく自由な発想を詰め込まれた、まさ
にNEO ZIPANGの世界。繁華街の真ん
中にあるマンションの5階に佇むその茶室は
驚きの異空間で、2010年度グッドデザイン
賞を受賞しています。

SHUHALLYの美しさの象徴とも言える小間
は、千利休が好んだと言われる黒で統一され
ています。床は漆黒の畳、壁や天井にはブ
ラックステンレスを使い、それらにLED照明
を内蔵し、人工光を現代的な要素として積極
的に取り入れながら、見事なまでの光と影の
空間を創り出しています。
また、茶器や茶道具など、様々な部分に、ス
トリートアートや現代美術作家の作品を取り
入れるなどして、新たな価値観や美意識を反
映した茶道具や茶室を創造しています。

SHUHALLY's own tea house 'Monsaian,'
named by 16th generation descendent of the
Urasenke tea house Zabosai, is packed with
original and free ideas that perfectly portray
the NEO ZIPANG world. Located on the 5th
floor of an apartment block on a busy street
in Yokohama, the tea house offers a stark
contrast from the outside world. It is a
recipient of the 2010 Good Design Award.

The 'koma' (small room) is a symbol of
SHUHALLY beauty, with a black tone
throughout in honor of Sen no Rikyu's love of
black. The tatami floor is lacquer black, and
black stainless steel used on the walls and
ceiling have LED lights embedded producing
a modern light effect that emphasizes the
contrast of light and shadow.
Works of art from street artists and other
contemporary artists feature in the bowls and
other tools, creating a new atmosphere and
aesthetic for tea ceremony customs and space.

NEO CULTURE:3 171

自らの価値観や美意識を反映する茶道の世界。その伝統の道に現代のライフスタイルが吹き込まれ、新たなスタイルが生まれつつあります。伝統に最新を掛け合わせることで生まれる新たな価値観が、日本の文化として未来へと繋がっていくのです。

Sado is said to be a reflection of your own values and aesthetic consciousness. That tradition has taken on a modern look, creating a new style of tea ceremony. Tradition crossed with innovation creates a new set of values that will lead Japan's culture into the future.

Information

SHUHALLY

神奈川県横浜市中区翁町1-3-18 松文ビル ルジャルダン横濱関内506号
JR京浜東北線・根岸線「関内駅」より徒歩3分
横浜市営地下鉄ブルーライン「関内駅」より徒歩7分
横浜市営地下鉄ブルーライン「伊勢佐木長者町駅」より徒歩8分
みなとみらい線「日本大通り駅」より徒歩8分

公式サイト https://shuhally.jp

【SHUHALLY】

Location: Le Jardin Yokohama Kannai room 506, Matsubun Bldg. 1-3-18 Okinacho, Nakaku, Yokohama City, Kanagawa Prefecture
3 minutes on foot from Kannai Station on the JR Keihin Tohoku Line or Negishi Line
7 minutes on foot from Kannai Station on the Yokohama Municipal Subway Blue Line
8 minutes on foot from Isezaki Chojamachi Station on the Yokohama Municipal Subway Blue Line
8 minutes on foot from Nihon Odori Station on the Minato Mirai Line

Official Website: https://shuhally.jp

歌舞伎

Ka
Bu
Ki

× 最新デジタル技術

KABUKI
×
LATEST DIGITAL TECHNOLOGY

A collaboration between the traditional Japanese stage performance
'*kabuki*' and advanced technology.
Discover a new depth to *kabuki*, unrestrained by convention
and incorporating trends and humor for everyone to enjoy.

Tradition × Innovation
NEO CULTURE

世界に誇る日本を代表する伝統芸能「歌舞伎」と、最新テクノロジーの融合。
既存の枠にとらわれず、流行や面白いものを取り入れ、
あらゆる人を楽しませる歌舞伎の奥深さがここにあります。

出演：中村獅童、初音ミク
©超歌舞伎 Supported by NTT

「歌舞伎」の由来は、「傾く（かぶく）」という言葉で、常軌を逸しているという意味があります。江戸時代初期に、一風変わった奇抜な格好や、世間の常識を逸した行動を好む「かぶき者」と呼ばれる若者たちがいました。そのかぶき者の姿を舞台に取り入れた「かぶき踊り」が歌舞伎のルーツと言われています。

The term '*kabuki*' originates from the *kanji* character 'to lean' and means to veer from the beaten track. In the early Edo Period, young people who dressed in eccentric clothes and went against the social norms were known as '*kabuki-mono*.' It is said that modern day *kabuki* began by portraying these *kabuki-mono* on stage.

400年以上の伝統を持つ、世界に誇る日本のポップカルチャー「歌舞伎」。ユネスコの無形文化遺産にも登録されている、日本を代表する伝統芸能のひとつです。

With a history of over 400 years, the UNESCO Intangible World Heritage '*kabuki*' is one of the better-known Japanese performance arts.

歌舞伎を成り立たせているのは文字通り、歌＝音楽、舞＝舞踊（踊り）、伎＝演技（芝居）です。
この三要素で、既存の枠にとらわれず、常に流行や面白いものを取り入れ、人々を楽しませながら磨き上げてきた「総合芸術」、それが歌舞伎なのです。

The *kanji* for *kabuki* (歌舞伎) have the following meanings: 歌 (ka)＝music, 舞 (bu)＝dance, 伎 (ki)＝performance. Using these three elements, *kabuki* creates a composite art form incorporating new elements with little regard for convention.

2016年には、「ニコニコ超会議」にて、最新のテクノロジーと歌舞伎の融合による、新しい歌舞伎が生まれました。その名も「超歌舞伎」。歌舞伎俳優の中村獅童さんとボーカロイドキャラクター（バーチャル・シンガー）の初音ミクが共演し、伝統芸能×テクノロジーのエキサイティングな舞台を実現させるという最新エンターテインメントです。

In 2016, a completely new form of *kabuki* merging tradition with advanced technology was premiered at Niconico Chokaigi, a gathering of Internet cultures hosted by video social website Niconico. This new *kabuki* is termed 'Cho-Kabuki.' Famous *kabuki* actor Shidou Nakamura teamed up with vocaloid virtual diva Hatsune Miku for a sensational performance merging tradition and technology.

舞台演出には日本最大の通信企業、「電話屋」ことNTTの技術をいかんなく発揮、舞台上で演じている歌舞伎俳優の姿だけを抜き出し、リアルタイムで別の場所に立体的に投影させることによる「分身の術」を実現させたり、下部モニターに初音ミク、上部モニターに背景を映し、装置内の鏡に反射させることで、正面からも背面からも初音ミクと背景を立体的に見られるようにする技術を取り入れた「山車」により、初音ミクがステージ上を練り歩くなど、臨場感満載の演出は、まさにNEO ZIPANGです。

The stage performance makes every use of telecommunications giant NTT's technology, taking images of a *kabuki* actor live on stage and beaming them to a separate location in real time. By showing Hatsune Miku on the lower monitor and the backdrop on the upper monitor, then flipping the image in an internalized mirror, the images can be seen in 3D from both the front and back. Watching the image of Hatsune Miku strutting back and forth on stage in front of your eyes epitomizes the essence of NEO ZIPANG.

さらに超歌舞伎の舞台は、「ニコニコ生放送」でリアルタイムに配信されます。生中継ならではの映像演出「AR（拡張現実）」が使用され、キャラクターが3Dでリアルに浮き出て見えたり、奥行きのある舞台で観ているような空間が演出されたり、会場とはまた違う楽しみ方ができるのです。2018年は、会場には2万人以上が来場し、ネットでの生放送は20万人以上が視聴したそうです。

Cho-Kabuki is broadcast live through the Niconico website, with augmented reality technology portraying the characters realistically in 3D making you feel as if you are actually by the stage. The real sense of depth offers a totally different yet somehow similar experience to actually being in the theatre. Over 20,000 people attended the 2018 event, with more than 200,000 tuning in online.

リアルとオンラインで、初めて歌舞伎を見る人から歌舞伎ファンまでを熱狂させてきた超歌舞伎。2019年夏には、歌舞伎発祥の地、京都南座でも公演。既存の枠にとらわれず、流行や面白いものを取り入れ、あらゆる人を楽しませるという歌舞伎の奥深さがここにあるのです。

Cho-Kabuki sent everyone who saw it live or online into a frenzy, from first timers to hard core *kabuki* fans. In 2019, *Cho-Kabuki* will return to Minamiza in Kyoto, the birthplace of *kabuki*. This original, trendy and interesting art form is set to impress on a new level.

Information

【超歌舞伎 オフィシャルサイト】
http://chokabuki.jp/

【歌舞伎美人（かぶきびと）】
https://www.kabuki-bito.jp/
歌舞伎公式総合サイト。歌舞伎の公演情報、ニュース、俳優インタビューなどがチェックできます。

【Cho-Kabuki Official Website】
http://chokabuki.jp/

【Kabuki-bito】
https://www.kabuki-bito.jp/
Official kabuki information
Find kabuki performance schedules, news and interviews with actors.

出演：中村獅童、初音ミク
©超歌舞伎 Supported by NTT

和太鼓 Wa Dai Ko

× プロジェクションマッピング

JAPANESE DRUMS × PROJECTION MAPPING

Ancient *wadaiko* (Japanese drums) are fused with the latest imaging technology.
'New Japanese Entertainment' turns the concept of *wadaiko* on its head,
touring 500 cities in 26 countries,
performing to an audience of eight million to high global acclaim.

Tradition × Innovation
NEO CULTURE
5

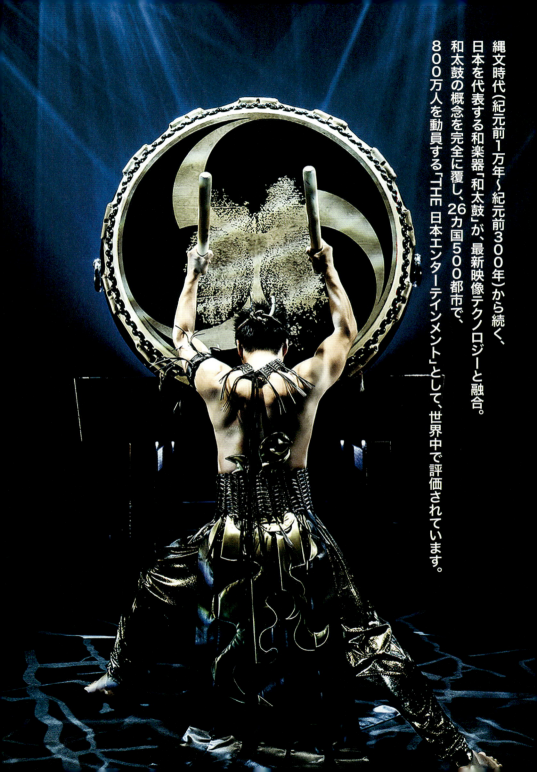

縄文時代（紀元前1万年〜紀元前300年）から続く、日本を代表する和楽器「和太鼓」が、最新映像テクノロジーと融合。和太鼓の概念を完全に覆し、26カ国500都市で、800万人を動員する「THE 日本エンターテインメント」として、世界中で評価されています。

日本を代表する和楽器「和太鼓」の歴史は非常に古く、縄文時代（紀元前1万年～紀元前300年）には、情報を伝達する手段として利用されていたと言われています。その後、様々な儀式や儀礼で使われたり、お祭りで演奏される「おはやし太鼓」として叩かれたり、戦国時代には軍の統率をとるために使われたり……。日本文化には欠かせない和太鼓の音は、日本人のソウルサウンドとも言えます。

Wadaiko, Japanese drums, date back to the Jomon Period, starting 10,000 years BC when they were used as a means of communication. Later they were adopted for various ceremonies and rituals and played at festivals. During the Sengoku period they were used to command armed forces.
The sound of *wadaiko* is the sound of Japanese culture, and a soul sound for many Japanese people.

日本にはいくつものプロの和太鼓集団があり、それぞれに素晴らしい個性を発揮していますが、ここでは、「DRUM TAO」を紹介します。「THE 日本エンターテインメント」として世界で称賛されている和太鼓集団で、圧倒的な音表現を持つ和太鼓と、美しい旋律の篠笛・三味線・箏などの驚異のパフォーマンスで、世界26カ国500都市での公演で観客動員数800万人に迫る公演実績を誇ります。
アクロバティックなパフォーマンス、伝統的かつ前衛的な迫力の和太鼓サウンド、圧倒的なヴィジュアルが特徴的で、常に新しい表現方法を生み出していくスタイルは、新しいアートパフォーマンスとして各国メディアから絶賛されています。

There are many professional drum groups in Japan, each with their own original and spectacular sounds. Of them all, DRUM TAO is possibly the best-known Japanese entertainment group around the world. Their powerful sound blended with melodies from beautiful bamboo flutes, *shamisen* and *koto* (traditional Japanese string instruments) create a spectacular performance that has mesmerized eight million people in 500 cities across 26 countries.
Acrobatic performances, powerfully traditional yet avant-garde sound and compelling visuals set this show apart. Their endless pursuit of new methods of artistic expression have garnered the attention of media worldwide.

2015年にはブロードウェイ・トニー賞4部門にノミネートされた制作チームがTAOのために再集結し、2016年にはオフ・ブロードウェイ進出を大成功（全6公演完売）させ、「TAOは日本を世界へ売り込む『顔』になる！」とニューヨーク・タイムズにて絶賛されました。

In 2015 a production team nominated for four categories of the Broadway Tony awards regrouped to team up with TAO, successfully carrying out six Off-Broadway shows in 2016. The New York Times lauded the shows, claiming 'TAO is the face of Japan.'

In 2017 a new show incorporating digital art, 'Mangekyo,' started in collaboration with ultra-technologist group TeamLab.
State-of-the-art projection mapping of Japanese aesthetics accompanies the powerful sound of *wadaiko* and beautiful melodies, resulting in a fantastical performance that destroys established norms of Japanese drums.
This traditional art that has been nurtured in Japan over centuries is adapted for the modern audience, creating a ground-breaking performance that merges tradition and innovation in what can only be called supreme entertainment.

2017年からは、デジタルアートのウルトラテクノロジスト集団・チームラボとタッグを組んで、映像演出を加えたショー「万華響 —MANGEKYO-」がスタートしました。
最新鋭映像のプロジェクトマッピングが日本美を映し出し、圧倒的な音表現を持つ和太鼓の美しいメロディーと融合する幻想的なパフォーマンスは、和太鼓の概念を完全に覆しています。
日本で脈々と培われてきた伝統芸術を、現代の人に受け入れられる形に進化させた最先端のパフォーマンスは、まさに「伝統と革新」が織り成す至高のエンターテインメントなのです。

Information

和太鼓エンタテインメント集団
『DRUM TAO』
◆オフィシャルサイト
http://www.drum-tao.com/

『万華響ーMANGEKYOー』
◆オフィシャルサイト
https://mangekyo-tokyo.com

Wadaiko entertainment group
"DRUM TAO"
Official Website
http://www.drum-tao.com/

"MANGEKYO"
Official Website
https://mangekyo-tokyo.com

日本の伝統楽器である津軽三味線、篠笛、鼓、そして西洋の伝統を受け継ぐヴァイオリンを融合させた和洋折衷の4人組バンド。日本を代表する伝統×最新サウンドは、すべてのシーンやジャンルを超えた世界を生み出します。

竜馬四重奏

「日本の伝統文化を音楽で世界に発信したい」との想いから、日本の伝統楽器である津軽三味線、篠笛、鼓、そして西洋の伝統を受け継ぐヴァイオリンを融合させた和洋折衷の4人からなるインストゥルメンタル・バンド「竜馬四重奏」は結成されました。

The Ryoma Quartet began with the desire to spread traditional Japanese culture and music to the world. They chose traditional instruments from Japan, along with the Western violin for their instrumental band.

ヴァイオリンの竜馬、津軽三味線の雅勝、篠笛の翠、鼓の仁、メンバー全員がそれぞれの楽器の世界では国内屈指の名プレイヤーであり、これまで様々なキャリアを経て、「自身が愛する伝統楽器をより多くの人に聴いてもらいたい。外に向けて発信していきたい」という強い想いと決意を持って演奏しています。

Ryoma on violin, Masakatsu on *shamisen*, Sui on *shinobue* and Zin on drums. Each a talented and distinguished musician in their own right, they have forged their own careers with the strong desire to share the instruments they love with more people, and promote their beloved sound.

オリジナリティ溢れる紋付袴の和式正装を身にまとい、竜馬四重奏が表現するのは、古典音楽をベースにEDM（エレクトロニック・ダンス・ミュージック）やポップス、ロック、ファンクなど現代的な音楽を取り入れた、新しい形のオリエンタルサウンドです。

Adorned in their unique crested *hakama* (Japanese traditional formal dress), the quartet performs an eclectic sound based on classical music with aspects of electronic dance music, pop, rock and funk, creating a totally new oriental sound.

その独自性がシーンやジャンルを超えて、2014年にはスペイン「日本スペイン交流400周年」3都市ツアー、2016年から4年連続で「JAPAN EXPO THAILAND」に出演、2018年のブルネイ、マレーシア公演など、日本国内外問わずオファーが絶えず世界各国から多大な支持を獲得しています。

Their distinctive sound is not defined by scenes or borders. They had three shows in Spain in 2014 to celebrate 400 years of exchange with Japan, performed four years straight at the JAPAN EXPO THAILAND, and held shows in Brunei and Malaysia in 2018. The quartet receive never-ending offers to perform in Japan and abroad, with a huge following worldwide.

「刀を伝統楽器に持ち替えた現代の侍」とも称される竜馬四重奏の奏でる音は、まさに、伝統から生まれる最新の音楽。"古くて新しい"彼らのメジャーデビューアルバム『NEO ZIPANG』。そしてセカンドアルバム『SAMURIZE』のタイトルどおり、それはまさに、日本を代表する伝統×最新サウンドです。

The Ryoma Quartet have been described as 'modern day samurai who have swapped swords for traditional instruments.' Their music is based on tradition but has a uniquely modern sound. Their major debut album 'NEO ZIPANG' and second album 'SAMURIZE' are evidence of this quartet's position representing Japan's traditional/innovative sound.

Information

『竜馬四重奏』オフィシャルサイト
http://ryoma-quartet.com/

Ryoma Quartet Official Website
http://ryoma-quartet.com/

●メジャーデビューアルバム『NEO ZIPANG』

●2nd アルバム『SAMURIZE』

●1stシングル『Sekai-Japan』

田んぼ×アート

Ta N Bo

RICE PADDIES × ART

Gigantic pictures and letters written on rice paddies are made possible through a collaboration of farming, art and technology. Japanese rice paddy art has garnered the attention of the world.

7

Tradition × Innovation
NEO CULTURE

風と共に去りぬ 田舎館村 2015年

田んぼをキャンバスにして、巨大な絵や文字を描き出すアート。農業×アート×テクノロジーのコラボレーションが、世界から注目されています。

ローマの休日（田舎館村 2018年）

1993年に青森県南津軽郡の田舎館村が村起こしの一環としてスタートさせた大地の芸術「田んぼアート」。田んぼをキャンバスにして色の異なる稲を植えることで巨大でありながらも繊細な絵や文字を描き出すこのアートは、日本全国に広まり、全国田んぼアートサミットも開催され、その芸術性の高さから海外メディアにも取り上げられるほど注目されています。

花魁とハリウッドスター（田舎館村 2013年）

Rice paddy art was first proposed in 1993, as part of an attempt by Inakadate, a small village in northern Japan, to boost interest and attention to their town. By planting different colored rice, huge pictures or letters can be 'grown' using rice fields as a 'canvas.' The spectacular results soon caught on and spread around Japan leading to the creation of a national rice field art summit, and garnering attention from international media too.

大いなる翼とナスカの地上絵（行田市、2018年）

198 NEO ZIPANG GYODA

桃太郎(田舎館村 2017年)

田んぼアートを見学するための展望施設等もあります。その場合は、斜め上から見られる前提で図案を設計し、遠近法を用いて植えられていたりもします。食用に広く栽培されているお米と、古代に栽培されていた古代米など何色もの稲を使用して、成長したときに田んぼに絵や文字を浮き出させています。稲が成長するにつれてだんだんと鮮明に現れてくるので、時期によって色合いの異なるアートが鑑賞できます。

竹取物語(田舎館村 2011年)

Special viewing platforms are set up to better view the rice paddy art. As they are not usually seen from directly above, the art must be planned accordingly, allowing for changes in perspective.
Using common short grain rice and different colored ancient varieties, the art only appears once the rice plants mature. As the rice grows, the intended effect slowly appears, then changes with passing time, allowing spectators to enjoy one piece of art through several stages.

未来へつなぐ古の軌跡（行田市、2015年）

2015年には、埼玉県行田市の田んぼアートが「最大の田んぼアート（Largest rice field mosaic）」として、ギネス世界記録に認定されました。総勢813人で苗を植えて描かれたアートのサイズは縦・横約165mの2万7,195㎡、25mプール約93面分です。ギネス世界記録に認定された2015年9月には、田んぼアートを見るために約4万人が訪れました。

In 2015, Gyoda City in Saitama set out to create the world's largest rice paddy mosaic. It took 813 people to plant the seedlings, creating a piece of art 165m by 165m, covering 27,000㎡, a world record recognized by Guinness. In September alone, around 40,000 people came to see the rice paddy spectacle.

恵比寿様と大黒様（田舎館村 2008年）

戦国武将とナポレオン（田舎館村 2009年）

200 NEO ZIPANG

富士山と羽衣伝説（田舎館村 2014年）

アートの枠を飛び越え、遂には、スマートフォンを用いて田んぼアートをQRコードのように読み取ることでお米が購入できる「rice-code」まで開発され、2014〜2015年に田舎館村で実証実験が行われました。これにより、田んぼアートを見に来た観光客がその場でお米を購入できるようになり、新たな販売手法として脚光を浴びました。この「rice-code」は、世界3大広告賞のひとつと言われるカンヌライオンズ・国際クリエイティビティ・フェスティバルで2部門の金賞を獲得し、海外からも注目されました。

Rice paddy art has now advanced even further, with the patterns creating a QR code that can be read with a smart phone, taking users to a site to purchase rice. After trials in Inakadate in 2014 and 2015, the 'rice-code' took off, allowing people who came to view the rice paddy art to order rice on the spot. This ingenious new 'rice-code' sales method drew much attention, winning gold in two categories at the Cannes Lions International Festival of Creativity, one of the largest advertising awards in the world.

イナタヒメノミコトとスサノオノミコト(行田市 2017年)

ヤマタノオロチとスサノオノミコト(田舎館村 2017年)

悲母観音と不動明王(田舎館村 2012年)

田んぼアートの見頃は、7月中旬〜8月中旬あたりですが、稲が育ち始める6月上旬から、稲の収穫前の10月前半までは観賞できます。育ち始めのうっすらした状態から、稲の色がはっきりと表れる夏、そして稲穂が実りセピア色に見える収穫前など、時期によって見え方が違うのも大きな魅力です。現地で見ると、稲が風で揺らぐことで、田んぼアートに動きが生まれ、写真とは違う立体感や迫力が楽しめます。

Prime season for viewing rice paddy art is from mid-June to mid-August, but it can be enjoyed from when the rice plants start growing in early June through to harvest in October. The images slowly start to appear as the rice grows, becoming clearest as the rice plants reach full height, then slowing changing colors to sepia as the rice matures. This continuous change is one of the great attractions of rice art. Seen first-hand, the stalks gently waving in the breeze give it a moving, 3D effect that can't be portrayed in photos.

Information

【田舎館村 田んぼアート】
田んぼアート発祥の地、青森県田舎館村の田んぼアートを見に行こう。

■田舎館村展望台（第1田んぼアート）
青森市より車で約60分／弘南鉄道「田舎館駅」より車で約5分／JR「川部駅」より車で約10分

■弥生の里展望所（第2田んぼアート）
青森市より車で約60分／弘南鉄道「田んぼアート駅」より徒歩すぐ

※「第一会場：田舎館村役場」と「第二会場：道の駅いなかだて・弥生の里展望所」に分かれています。
※田んぼアートの期間中は第1田んぼアートと第2田んぼアートを結ぶシャトルワゴンが無料で運行しています。

最新の情報は公式サイトなどでご確認ください。
http://www.inakadate-tanboart.net

【行田市 田んぼアート】
世界最大の田んぼアートを生み出した、埼玉県行田市の田んぼアートを見に行こう。

■古代蓮の里：古代蓮会館展望室
東北自動車道 羽生ICより車で約25分、加須ICより車で約30分
関越自動車道 東松山ICより車で約40分、花園ICより車で約60分
JR「行田駅」より市内循環バス「古代蓮の里」下車で約25分

【Inakadate-mura rice paddy art】
Visit the birthplace of rice paddy art,
Inakadate-mura in Aomori Prefecture.

■ Inakadate observation platform (first venue)
60 minutes by car from Aomori City
5 minutes by car from Inakadate Station on the
Konan line
10 minutes by car from JR Kawabe Station

■ Yayoi no Sato observation platform (second venue)
60 minutes by car from Aomori City
Directly beside Tanboart Station on the Konan
line

※Venue one is by Inakadate Village Hall and
venue two is by Michinoeki Inakadate.
During the art event, a free shuttle runs
between the two venues.

Latest information can be found on the official
website.
http://www.inakadate-tanboart.net

【Gyoda City Rice Paddy Art】
Visit the sight of the world's largest rice paddy
art in Gyoda City, Saitama.

■ Kodaihasu observation tower
25 minutes by car from Hanyu IC, 30 minutes from
Kazo IC on the Tohoku expressway
40 minutes from Higashimatsuyama IC, 60 minutes
from Hanazono IC on the Kanetsu Expressway
25 minutes by bus from JR Gyoda Station, get off at
Kodaihasu no Sato.

竹 × 照明デザイン
BAMBOO × LIGHTING DESIGN

Bamboo has long supported the Japanese way of life.
It has now been combined with lighting and design to create fantastic new art
'bamboo lighting,' connecting people to people,
people to places, and people to nature.

Tradition × Innovation
NEO CULTURE

日本の暮らしを支え続けてきた竹に、あかりとデザインを掛け合わせて生まれた幻想的アート「竹あかり」。「人と人・人とまち・人と自然」を繋ぐ竹あかりは、新たな日本文化を生み出します。

日本の暮らしを支え続けてきた竹。縄文時代の遺跡から竹を素材とした製品が出土しており、日本人と竹の関わりの歴史は非常に古いと言われています。カゴや箸といった日用品から、建築やインテリアの資材、農耕具、玩具などにも利用され、さらには、日本文化である茶道や華道の道具、尺八や笛などの楽器、竹刀や弓といった武道具にも用いられている竹は、日本人の文化と生活に深い関わりを持つ万能な植物なのです。

Bamboo has long been a cornerstone of the Japanese lifestyle. Bamboo artefacts have been discovered dating back to the Jomon Period (beginning 14,000 years BC), evidence of the long history Japanese have of using bamboo. From baskets to chopsticks, buildings to furniture, farming tools to toys, bamboo has a place in all facets of Japanese life. It plays a central role in many aspects of Japanese culture such as *sado* (tea ceremony) and *kado* (flower arrangement), musical instruments such as the *shakuhachi* (Japanese bamboo clarinet) and flutes, and even has a place in martial arts such as kendo and Japanese archery. This versatile plant is indispensable to life in Japan.

熊本県のアート集団「ちかけん」は、竹から広がる幻想的なあかりを使って、日本中のお祭りをプロデュースしたり、百貨店のショーウィンドウ、ウェディングやクリスマス、野外フェスといった様々なイベントで空間を演出したりしています。2016年に開催された先進国首脳会議「伊勢志摩サミット」では、会場演出と竹あかり制作のワークショップを担当し、世界からも注目されています。

'Chikaken,' an artist group from Kumamoto Prefecture, make use of the fantastical light from bamboo lighting at festivals, department store displays, weddings, Christmas decorations and outdoor music festivals throughout Japan. During the G-7 Ise-Shima Summit in 2016, Chikaken set up lighting displays and ran a bamboo light making workshop, receiving attention from around the world.

CHIKAKEN × canaarea × T.BANBUS 共作

日本人にとって身近な存在である竹に、あかりとデザインを掛け合わせることによって、「竹あかり」という幻想的なアートが誕生しました。竹に穴を開け、ろうそくやLEDであかりを灯すことで生み出される幻想的な世界。優しい光と影が溶け合い、様々な表情を魅せてくれる竹あかりは、息をのむほど美しく、多くの人に感動を与えています。

By crossing this familiar material with lighting and design, a new, fantastic art 'bamboo lighting' was born.
Candles and LED lights shining through holes cut in bamboo create a fantastical world. The gentle light dissolves into shadows creating a range of expressions, many of them breathtakingly beautiful.

竹あかりは、ただ美しいだけではありません。時代が進むにつれて竹の需要が減り、放置される竹林が増えることで生態系が乱れている「竹害」と呼ばれる問題の解決にも一役買っているのです。厄介者として扱われている竹にデザインを与えることで、資源として価値を見出し、地域を盛り上げるための資源として活用し、最後には、竹炭にして土に還す活動をしています。
竹あかりは、「持続可能な社会づくり」というメッセージを持った芸術作品でもあるのです。

Bamboo lighting is not only good for aesthetic beauty. As demand for bamboo wanes, bamboo forests have slowly encroached on surrounding ecosystems. Regular harvesting keeps the bamboo under control and the ecosystems in balance. Often considered a nuisance, by giving bamboo a use with good design, it becomes an important resource, stimulating the local economy. When bamboo has finished its useful life, it is turned into charcoal and returned to the earth. Bamboo lighting is an art form that carries a message for creating a sustainable society.

「竹あかり」という作品を通し、世界中に日本の芸術性を表現するとともに、環境問題に立ち向かい、人と人の和を築き、地域の活性化に繋げていく「ちかけん」の活動は、新たな日本文化をつくっていくに違いありません。

Through bamboo lighting, Chikaken have introduced a uniquely Japanese art to the world, while working to solve environmental problems, bring people together and stimulate rural communities. Their work is sure to create a new Japanese culture to be proud of.

Information

ちかけん　CHIKAKEN
竹あかり総合演出
「ちかけん」のオフィシャルサイト
http://chikaken.com/

【CHIKAKEN】
Bamboo lighting producers Chikaken, official website
http://chikaken.com/

NEO CULTURE:8　211

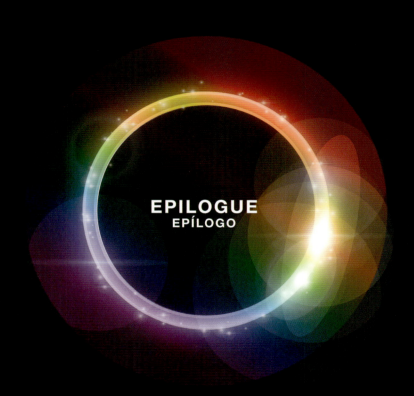

ÜSA's DREAM NOTE

ウサが進行中のプロジェクトを紹介

Current projects with author / performer ÜSA

Üsa introduce sus proyectos en curso

This is my DREAM NOTE...

僕は、若い頃から旅とダンスが好きで、世界を旅しながら踊り続けています。
もちろん、楽しいことばっかりじゃなかったけど、
多くの素晴らしい人に出逢い、本当に多くのことを、学ばせてもらいました。

そして、この本を読んでくれた人はご存じの通り！
日本だって、ぜんぜん、世界に負けてないですよね。

僕らの生まれた日本に溢れる素晴らしいもの、
そして、自分自身の中から溢れてくる熱いパッションを、
世界に向けて、どんどん発信していきたい！
その表現を通して、世界中のひとりでも多くの人が喜んだり、
元気になってくれたら、サイコーすぎる！

そんな気持ちで、現在、いくつかのプロジェクトを進めています。
まだまだ、夢の段階で、ドリームノートではありますが、せっかくの機会なので、
この本のエピローグとして、3つのプロジェクトを紹介したいと思います。

僕ひとりでは、叶えられない夢ばかりです。
興味があったら、ぜひ、一緒に進めていければと想っています。
楽しんでいきましょう！　Come join us!

EXILE ÜSA

► English

I have always loved traveling and dancing, and still enjoy traveling the world to dance.
Admittedly, there were hard times amongst the fun, but I met many wonderful people, and learned many important things along the way.
As you have hopefully come to realize through this book, Japan also has many wonderful things to boast about.
I want to share all the wonderful things in our country Japan to the world, along with the passion and energy I have boiling up inside!
By expressing and sharing these things, I hope to bring joy and energy to more and more people around the world.
It's with this passion that I started a number of projects I'd like to introduce.
While some are still in the dream stage, hence the title 'ÜSA's dream,' I want to take this opportunity to introduce three of them in this epilogue.
I can't achieve any of these dreams alone.
If you're interested, then please come along and join the fun!

EXILE ÜSA

► Español

Desde joven me han gustado los viajes y el baile, por lo que he continuado viajando y bailando. Ciertamente no todo ha sido diversión, pero he conocido a gente extraordinaria y realmente he podido aprender muchas cosas.

Y Japón de ninguna manera se queda atrás, ¡Como saben quiénes hayan leído este libro!

¡Quiero ir difundiendo al mundo todo lo maravilloso que hay en Japón, donde yo nací, así como la ferviente pasión que surge de mí! Y si a través de mi expresión, mucha gente en todo el mundo llegara a sentir alegría y energía, ¡Eso sería más que lo máximo!

Con este espíritu es que actualmente estoy impulsando algunos proyectos. Aún se trata de notas sobre mis sueños, pero quisiera introducirles tres proyectos.

Todos ellos son sueños que no podré realizar yo solo. Si les interesa, desearía que los impulsáramos juntos. ¡Únete a nosotros!

ÜSA DE EXILE

PROJECT: 01

NEO ZIPANG

ネ オ ジ パ ン グ

PROJECT: 01
NEO ZIPANG
▷ A new genre of music and dance… from Japan!
▷ ¡Por un nuevo género de música y baile lanzado desde Japón!

DREAM NOTE
PRESENTED BY ÜSA

PROJECT ①
ネオジパング

NEO ZIPANG

日本発信！
音楽・ダンスの新しいジャンルを。

A new genre of music and dance... from Japan!

¡Por un nuevo género de música
y baile lanzado desde Japón!

DANCE EARTH

2006年から、「DANCE EARTH / 地球で踊ろう」というテーマを掲げ、世界数十カ国を旅しながら、現地の人々の暮らしに触れ、現地のダンサーに教わり、ときにはバトルもしながら、世界中の踊りを体験してきました。
そして、2015〜2018年にかけて、日本国内のお祭りを巡り、素晴らしい伝統的な音と踊りを、いっぱい体験させてもらいました。
世界を巡り、日本を巡り、踊り続けながら‥‥僕は、実感しました。

日本人は、いつも、物静かで、シャイなわけじゃない。
日本には、世界に誇れる、かっこいい音楽、踊りが溢れてる!
日本に古くから伝わる音楽と踊りを、現代風にアレンジして、HIPHOP、ROCK、JAZZのような、ひとつのジャンルとして、世界中に発信したら、きっと、すごいことになる!

Since 2006 I have traveled the world with the motto 'DANCE EARTH,' visiting dozens of countries to sample the lives of local people, learn from local dancers (and occasionally have dance battles with them) and experience the different dance styles of the world.
From 2015 to 2018 I traveled around Japan, touring festivals around the country to learn and experience all the wonderful traditional sounds and dances of this country.
Dancing my way around Japan and the world, I came to realize a few important things.
Japanese people aren't always quiet and shy. Japan actually boasts a host of cool music and dances that we can share with the world.
If we can add a contemporary touch to traditional Japanese music and dance, morphing it into some new genre much like how hip-hop, rock and jazz were created, I'm sure it will make a huge impact on the world.

A partir del 2006 he estado viajando por decenas de países bajo el tema "DANCE EARTH. / Bailar el mundo", teniendo contacto con la vida de la gente en otros países, aprendiendo de los bailarines locales e incluso compitiendo con ellos en ocasiones, a fin de experimentar los bailes de todo el mundo. Y entre el 2015 y el 2018 recorrí los festivales tradicionales (Omatsuri) en Japón, teniendo la oportunidad de experimentar las estupendas tradiciones sonoras y de baile. Al recorrer el mundo y recorrer Japón... yo me percaté de algo.

Los japoneses no siempre son silenciosos y tímidos. ¡Japón está repleto de música y baile de la que puede enorgullecerse ante el mundo! Si se lograra arreglar de forma contemporánea la música y baile que se ha heredado desde tiempos remotos en Japón, para crear un solo género como el HIPHOP, ROCK o JAZZ y transmitirlo al mundo, ¡eso tendría un gran impacto!

NEO ZIPANG=NEO CULTURE

NEW DANCE
NUEVO BAILE

NEW MUSIC
NUEVA MÚSICA

NEW FASHION
NUEVA MODA

そして、日本発信の新しい音楽と踊りのジャンルを生み出そうと、動き始めました。
その名も、「NEO ZIPANG / ネオジパング」。
そう、この本のタイトルにもある通り、今でも、日本は、黄金の国です。

まず、世界に通じるジャンルが生まれるために、必要な要素は、主に3つです。
それは、新しい「音」、新しい「踊り」、そして、新しい「ファッション」。
伝統×最新をうまくミックスしながら、日本独自の魅力を発信するために。
現在、心ある職人さんやアーティストたちと共に、切磋琢磨しながら、試作を重ねています。

With this in mind, I set out to create a new genre of music and dance from Japan called NEO ZIPANG.
That's right, as you know from the title of this book, Japan is still a country of gold.
To create a genre that will catch on around the world, we need to work on three main elements:
New sound, new dance, and new fashion.
With the right mix of tradition and innovation, we can promote to the world a new image of Japan.
I'm currently working with like-minded artists and craftspeople in a process of trial and error to achieve this very goal.

ué así que comencé a moverme aspirando a crear un nuevo género de música y baile lanzado desde Japón. Su nombre es "NEO ZIPANG". En efecto, Japón sigue siendo el país dorado.

En primer lugar, hay 3 elementos principales para que nazca un género que sea reconocido en el mundo. Éstos son, un nuevo "sonido", un nuevo "baile" y una nueva "moda". Para transmitir lo singularmente atractivo de Japón, mezclando tradición con lo más moderno, actualmente estamos haciendo varios ensayos con esmero, en conjunto con artesanos y artistas.

NEW DANCE
NUEVO BAILE
NEW MUSIC
NUEVA MÚSICA

新しい音と踊りを生み出すときに、大きなヒントにしているのは、日本中に溢れる素敵な「祭り」です。日本には、約30万もの祭りがあると言われていますが、特にインスピレーションを受けたのは、HIPHOPとの親近感を感じた、「徳島の阿波おどり」、そして、輪になって踊る、「各地の盆踊り」の独特な動きです。
日本の歴史上、ずっと、愛されてきた音や踊りを基本に、僕なりの感性でアレンジを加えながら、お祭り独特の興奮を世界中で再現できたらと思っています。

One major inspiration for this new genre of sound and dance is the variety of wonderful festivals held around Japan. Of the approximately 300,000 different festivals held around the country, I was particularly taken by the hip-hop like feel of Tokushima's 'awa-odori', and the myriad of circular 'bon' dances performed around the country with distinctive movements.
Based on these beloved sounds and dances that have evolved through the history of Japan, I have added my own original aspects in an attempt to recreate the unique excitement of Japanese festivals and share it with the world.

Lo que considero una gran clave para crear un nuevo sonido y baile son los maravillosos festivales "Matsuri" que hay en todo Japón. Se afirma que en Japón hay alrededor de 300 mil festivales "Matsuri", y los que me han servido especialmente de inspiración, son "Awaodori de Tokushima" del que percibí cierta cercanía con el HIPHOP, así como los movimientos particulares de los "bon-odori de cada región". Tomando como base los sonidos y bailes que la gente ha amado a lo largo de la historia de Japón, quisiera agregar arreglos de mi inspiración a fin de recrear y transmitir en todo el mundo la emoción propia de los festivales "Matsuri".

NEW FASHION
Nueva moda

新しいファッションを生み出すときも、基本の考えは同じです。日本の素晴らしいもの×世界を旅しながら得た僕なりの感性で、和服、浴衣、着物などを、踊れる衣装としてアレンジします。

特に影響を受けているのは、戦国時代のアウトローや不良たちが愛した「傾く（かぶく）」精神を受け継ぎ、「歌舞く（かぶく）」クリエイションを続けている世界的デザイナー・プロデューサーの山本寛斎さん。寛斎さんの遊び心を大切にしながら、不可能と思われることを、なんでも可能にしちゃう元気なエネルギーに僕は心底惚れていて、これからも一緒に、世界中の人が驚くようなカラフルなファッションやパフォーマンスを生み出していきたいと思っています。

The same fundamentals apply to creating new fashion. Taking the best of Japanese traditions and applying the knowledge and international sense I've garnered through my travels, I'm able to arrange Japanese traditional dresses such as *yukata* and *kimono* into costumes for dancing. World renowned designer and producer Kansai Yamamoto has been a huge influence in this aspect. Kansai carries on the legacy of Japanese outlaws from the Sengoku Period and their penchant to '*kabuku*,' or buck trends. His playful style helps make the seemingly impossible, possible, and his energy is something I admire from the bottom of my heart. Kansai is someone I rely on to help create colorful fashion and performances that take the world by surprise.

Para crear una nueva moda, también trabajo con la misma idea básica. Basándome en "lo maravilloso que hay en Japón" multiplicado por "la percepción que obtuve viajando por el mundo", diseño atuendos para bailar con una combinación de kimono, yukata, etc.
En especial he recibido inspiración del diseñador mundialmente conocido Kansai Yamamoto, que continúa realizando la creación "Kabuku", heredera del espíritu "Kabuku" que gustaba a los las personas fuera de la ley y los rebeldes del Periodo Sengoku. Yo estoy enamorado de la energía de Kansai que hace posible lo imposible dándole importancia a la creatividad, y quisiera crear en conjunto una moda colorida que asombre a las personas del mundo.

NEO ZIPANG
FROM JAPAN

日本発信の新しい音楽・踊りのジャンル「NEO ZIPANG」。
これが、世界中のクラブで流れ、ヒットチャートに登場して、このジャンルを通して、世界中の若者たちが、「日本って、カッコイイ！ COOL！」ってシャウトしてくれる日を夢見て、一緒に、盛り上がっていきましょう！

NEO ZIPANG: A new genre of music and dance from Japan.
I dream of the day this music blasts from dance clubs around the world, topping hit charts and prompting young people around the world to shout, 'Japan? Cool!' Join me in creating this new history of NEO ZIPANG!

"NEO ZIPANG", el nuevo género de música y baile lanzado desde Japón. Démosle vida juntos a este género, soñando con el día en que suene en todas las discotecas del mundo, aparezca en las listas de popularidad y los jóvenes de todo el mundo alcen la voz diciendo "¡Japón es cool!"

FRIENDS

山本寛斎

このNEO ZIPANG構想で、絶対に外せない存在である山本寛斎さん。

71年、ロンドンにおいて日本人として初めてファッション・ショーを開催、世界の舞台に踊り出た。これ以降、デヴィッド・ボウイ、エルトン・ジョン、スティーヴィー・ワンダーらとの交流が始まる。既成概念を突き崩すアヴァンギャルドなデザインは、時代に敏感な若者から圧倒的な支持を獲得した。74年から92年までパリ・ニューヨーク・東京コレクションに参加し、世界的デザイナーとしての地位を築く。93年以降は、ファッションデザイナーの枠を超え、スペクタクルなライブイベントのプロデューサーとして活躍。世界中でKANSAI SUPER SHOWや日本元気プロジェクトを開催し、総動員数は360万人以上にのぼる。2008年G8洞爺湖サミットの会場・社交行事の総合プロデュース、成田新高速鉄道の特急「京成スカイライナー」新型車両の内装・外装のデザイン(2010年度グッドデザイン賞、2011年度ブルーリボン賞受賞)担当、2016年から2018年まで熊本県山鹿市の「山鹿灯籠まつり」アドバイザーを務めるなど、幅広いジャンルで活躍中。

「歌舞く」精神を根底に活動を続ける日本が誇るトップクリエイターである山本寛斎さんには、様々な面でご協力いただいています!
寛斎さんが監督総指揮を務めるファッションとアートのイベント「日本元気プロジェクト」にパフォーマーとして出演させていただいたり、DANCE EARTH PARTYとして発表した楽曲『NEO ZIPANG 〜 UTAGE 〜』では、メンバー衣裳をプロデュースしていただいたり。
これからも、NEO ZIPANGの世界を一緒に広げていければと思っています。

FRIENDS

Kansai Yamamoto

Kansai Yamamoto is an indispensable part of the NEO ZIPANG initiative.

Kansai Yamamoto was the first Japanese to hold a fashion show in London, announcing his arrival on the world stage in 1971. This set up his relationship with such famous musicians as David Bowie, Elton John and Stevie Wonder. His avant-garde designs show little regard for convention, earning a strong following from fashion-conscious youth. From 1974 to 1992 he featured in the Paris, New York, and Tokyo Collections, earning a reputation as a world-leading designer. From 1993 he branched out from fashion design into producing spectacular live events. He has entertained over 3.6 million guests at his worldwide KANSAI SUPER SHOW and Nippon Genki Project. In 2008 he was put in charge of venue and social event production at the G8 Toyako Summit. He designed both the interior and exterior of the new Narita Rapid Rail express train 'Skyliner,' scooping up the 2010 Good Design award 2011 Blue Ribbon award in the process. From 2016 to 2018 he was advisor for the Yamaga Toro festival in Kumamoto, and continues to influence a wide variety of fields with his creativity.

Japan's leading designer Kansai Yamamoto has lent his time and energy to various aspects of this project, bringing his devotion to the rebellious '*kabuku*' spirit.
I have performed at his fashion and art event Nippon Genki Project, and he has produced costumes for the new song NEO ZIPANG ~UTAGE~ at the DANCE EARTH PARTY.
I look forward to spreading the NEO ZIPANG world together with him.

AMIGOS

Kansai Yamamoto

En este proyecto NEO ZIPANG es imprescindible la presencia de Kansai Yamamoto.

Fué el primer japonés en realizar un desfile de modas en Londres en 1971, apareciendo así en la escena mundial. A partir de ello comenzó a relacionarse con David Bowie, Elton John y Stevie Wonder. Sus diseños vanguardistas que derrumbaron los conceptos preconcebidos recibieron un gran apoyo de los jóvenes, que son sensibles con la época. De 1974 a 1992 participó en las colecciones de París, Nueva York y Tokio, consolidando su estatus como un diseñador de prestigio mundial. A partir de 1993 cruzó las barreras de diseñador de modas, convirtiéndose en productor de espectáculos en vivo. En todo el mundo ha organizado "KANSAI SUPER SHOW" y "NIPPON GENKI PROYECT"a Los que han acudido más de 3.6 millones de personas. También ha realizado una variedad de trabajos incluyendo el diseño general del foro y los eventos sociales de la Cumbre del G8 en Toyako, el diseño interior y exterior del nuevo modelo del tren express "Keisei Skyliner" al Aeropuerto de Narita (ganador de los premios Good Design 2010 y Blue Ribbon 2011), además de fungir como asesor del festival ""Yamaga Tourou Matsuri (festival de linternas de Yamaga), en la ciudad de Yamaga, Prefectura de Kumamoto, del 2016 al 2018.

Kansai Yamamoto, uno de los principales creadores y orgullo de Japón, que continúa activo teniendo como base el espíritu "Kabuku", ¡También ha colaborado en varias facetas del proyecto! Nos ha permitido presentarnos como parte del evento de moda y arte "NIPPON GENKI PROYECT", del que Kansai es director general, además de producir el atuendo en la presentación de la canción "NEO ZIPANG-UTAGE" en el evento "DANCE EARTH PARTY". Deseamos seguir difundiendo en conjunto con Kansai el mundo de NEO ZIPANG.

DREAM NOTE
PRESENTED BY ÜSA

DANCE LANGUAGE
Idioma del baile

PROJECT: 02

Using dance to create a new global language.

Por un idioma utilizable
en todo el mundo a través del baile

PROJECT ②
ダンス語

Dance Language

ダンスを活かして、
世界中で使える新しい言語を。

Using dance to create a new global language.

Por un idioma utilizable en todo el mundo a través del baile

DANCE LANGUAGE

原始時代から変わらない「踊り」という世界共通の表現を通して、国境も宗教も言語も肌の色も超えて、人と人が、心と心が、繋がっていく、「新しい言葉」を創ってみたい。少しでも、DANCEで世界をハッピーにしたい！
そんな想いで始まったのが、この「ダンス語」プロジェクトです。

そして、このダンス語を通して、「おもいやり」「おもてなし」「もったいない」などの和の精神であったり、沖縄の「ゆいま〜る」「いちゃりばちょーでー」、アイヌの言語で「イランカラプテ」（あなたの心にそっと触れさせていただきます、の意）など、日本の各地域に残っている素敵なスピリッツも、世界に広げていきたいと思っています。

Dance has been a part of life in all cultures around the world since primeval times, regardless of region, religion, language or skin color.
I want to create a 'new language' that brings people together, connecting their hearts.
"To make the world a happier place through dance," that is the idea behind my Dance Language project.

Through this dance language, I want to take the Japanese ideals of '*omoiyari*' (consideration), '*omotenashi*' (hospitality) and '*mottainai*' (not wasting), along with wonderful local ideals from around Japan such as '*yuima-ru*' (mutual aid) and '*ichari bacho-de*' (we're all related) from Okinawa and the Ainu '*irankarapte*' (I will gently touch your heart) from northern Japan, and share them with the world.

Quisiera intentar crear un "nuevo idioma" en el que las personas y los corazones se entrelacen superando las fronteras, religiones, lenguas y el color de la piel, a través de la expresión del "baile" que es común en el mundo y que no ha cambiado desde la prehistoria. ¡Quisiera hacer que en el mundo haya aunque sea un poco más de felicidad a través del baile! Con esta idea es que comenzó este proyecto del "idioma del baile".

Y a través de este idioma del baile quisiera difundir en el mundo el magnífico espíritu que aún existe en varias regiones de Japón, incluyendo el espíritu japonés del "omoiyari" (ser atento), "omotenashi" (hospitalidad) y "mottainai" (no malgastar recursos), así como el espíritu de Okinawa de "yuimaaru" (ayudarse mutuamente), "icharibachoodee" (si nos encontramos una vez somos hermanos) y en idioma ainu "irankaraputa" (permítame tocar un poco su corazón).

Dance Language

Dance Language

「おいしい」
Delicious / Delicioso

まずは、1発目ということで、「おいしい！」のダンスを踊ってきました。
飢餓をなくすことを目標に活動している国連WFP（世界食糧計画）のサポーターとして、カリブ海に面する素敵な国、ホンジュラスに行って、現地の子どもたちと一緒に過ごしながら、「おいしい！」という気持ちを、踊りと踊りで交換してきました。

「おいしい！」に続いて、「いただきます」「うれしい」「ありがとう」「え？ なんて言ったの？」などなど……
そんなダンス語も、現在、制作中です。

To get things started, I began with the 'yummy' dance.
I visited the wonderful Caribbean country of Honduras as a supporter of the WFP (World Food Programme), a UN program aiming to eradicate hunger, and spent time with children there creating and exchanging dances to express 'yummy'.
After 'yummy' came 'itadakimasu' (let's eat with appreciation for food), 'happy,' 'thanks,' 'what did you say?' and many more.
I'm still working on more of this dance language.

Como primer intento, hemos bailado el baile de "¡delicioso!".
Como promotor del Programa Mundial de Alimentos de la ONU, cuyo objetivo es acabar con el hambre, fuí a Honduras, un bello país que colinda con el Caribe, donde pasé el tiempo con los niños locales y realicé intercambios de baile expresando "¡delicioso!".

Tras "¡delicioso!", actualmente estoy creando el idioma del baile de "buen provecho", "felicidad", "gracias", "¿Qué dijiste?", etcétera.

ÜSA's DREAM NOTE 235

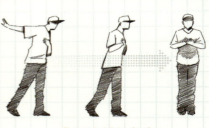
「ありがとう」
Thank you / Gracias

「いただきます」
Eat with gratitude
Gracias por la comida (al empezar a comer)

まずは、ダンス語の言葉数を、100個くらいまで増やせたら、最低限、生活に必要な気持ちは伝えられるようになると思うので、現在は、それを目指して、日々、クリエイト中です。100個のダンス語が完成次第、WEBで誰もが見られるようにしたり、ガイドブックを制作しようと企んでいます。

「うれしい」
Happy / Feliz

「え？ 何て言ったの？」
Huh? What did you say? / ¿Qué? ¿Qué dijiste?

そして、言葉の数が増えるのはいいけど、もちろん、使ってもらわないと意味がありません。まずは、僕らが国内・海外で運営しているダンススクールをスタートに、世界中のダンススクール、インターナショナルスクールなどに広げていきたいと想っています。さらに、ダンス語だけで伝わる曲・PVも創っていきます。

Dance Language

If I can create around 100 basic expressions through dance language, that will allow me to get by in everyday situations. That is my current and immediate goal. Once these 100 'dance words' are ready, I'll release them on the Internet for everyone to see, and plan to make a guidebook too.

And it's not enough to just create the language; it needs to be used too. I'll start introducing the dance language to dance schools I manage around the world, expanding to other dance schools and international schools. Eventually, I want to make new songs and promotional videos using just dance language.

En un principio, supongo que si pudiera aumentar hasta unas 100 las palabras del idioma del baile se podrían expresar las sensaciones necesarias en la vida cotidiana, por lo que actualmente me dedico a la creación todos los días aspirando a ello. Cuando complete las 100 palabras del idioma del baile, planeo difundirlas en internet para que todos las puedan ver, y además planeo editar una guía.

Además de que es bueno que cada vez haya más palabras, ciertamente no tendrá sentido si no son utilizadas. Por ello estoy pensando difundirlas en las escuelas de baile y escuelas internacionales de todo el mundo comenzando por las escuelas de bailes administradas por nosotros en Japón y en el extranjero. Además crearemos canciones y videos promocionales utilizando sólo el idioma del baile.

夢としては、多くの著名なダンサーたちにも協力してもらいながら、世界中にダンス語が広まり、最終的には、世界中の旅人たちが、このダンス語で、いろんな気持ちを交換して、友達になったり、恋に落ちたりする日が来たら嬉しいな、と思っています。
このプロジェクトに、興味がある方は、ぜひ、ご連絡を！
一緒に楽しんでいきましょう！

My dream is to collaborate with many famous dancers, spreading dance language around the world so that travelers from any country can communicate and share their feelings, making new friends and perhaps even falling in love.
If you are interested in becoming a part of this project, please get in touch.
Let's have fun together!

Mi sueño consiste en que el idioma del baile sea difundido por todo el mundo con la cooperación de bailarines famosos, concibiendo que sería una dicha que al final los viajeros de todo el mundo intercambien sentimientos con este idioma del baile, se hagan amigos e incluso lleguen a enamorarse. Quienes estén interesados en este proyecto, ¡por favor contacten conmigo! ¡Divirtámonos juntos!

FRIENDS

FATIMATA（ファティマタ）

西アフリカ、セネガルの伝統舞踊『サバールダンス』やガーナのダンス『アゾントダンス』の魅力を日本に広めたパイオニア。2008年はEXILE ÜSAのセネガル渡航をコーディネートし、2010年の劇団EXILEの『Dance Earth』の舞台でサバールダンスの振り付けを担当。2012年はNHK Eテレの『Eダンスアカデミー』の番組でセネガルの部族語『ウォロフ語』の通訳者として出演。2016年は同番組にてキッズにアゾントダンスをレクチャーし、ガーナの食やファッションなども紹介。同番組でコーナー化した『きょうのアゾント』の監修を務めた。2017年はÜSAプロデュースのユニット『DANCE EARTH PARTY』のファーストアルバムに収録されている『AZONTO』の振付けを担当。10月に行われた『DANCE EARTH FESTIVAL 2017』にて『AZONTO』を披露した。2019年は『Eダンスアカデミー』の番組にてコーナー化している『あいうえおダンス』の振り付け監修を担当している。
現在は、国際交流イベントやフェスなどを中心にダンスパフォーマンスやトークショー、ワークショップなどで陽気で華やかなアフリカの文化を伝え、西アフリカから仕入れた色鮮やかなファブリックの雑貨や服飾の販売なども行い、アフリカのおしゃれ文化の発信も精力的に行なっている。

FATIMATAさんが得意とするガーナのダンス『アゾントダンス』は、日常で起きていることをダンスで表現しながら、みんながコミュニケーションを取るという踊り。
ダンス語を一緒に考えるメンバーとして、FATIMATAさんはピッタリ！　ということで仲間になってもらいました。

田中新

フラダンス教室｜ハーラウ・ケオラクーラナキラ主宰。
ハワイの人間国宝が最後に認めた唯一の日本人フラ指導者。
エッカードカレッジ（フロリダ・米）にて国際関係学を専攻後、ハワイ大学マノア校大学院にて文化人類学を専攻。ハワイと日本の文化を研究し帰国後、ハワイの人間国宝である故ジョージ・ナオペに本格的にフラを教わり、2003年〜 2019年現在、生前彼の右腕として全幅の信頼を寄せたクムフラ（フラ指導者）エトア・ロペスに師事。日本ではインストラクターとして11年間（2002-2013）母親のフラ教室に所属し、国内外の競技会で活躍。2013年には、フラで最も権威のある大会第50回メリーモナークフラフェスティバルにおいて、エトア・ロペス主宰フラハーラウ・ナー・プア・ウイ・オ・ハワイのホオパア（ドラム）として日本人初の大役を務めた。同年母の教室を独立後、【フラ】を通じて「毎日をもっと笑顔に、より彩りのある日常を」目指して、麻布十番を本拠地に自身のフラ教室を主宰。2018年教室主催の第一回発表会を開催。2019年現在約50名以上の男性が所属する日本でも随一のフラ教室へと発展。
彼の振付は【踊る】というよりもむしろ、自然そのものを体現しているようだ。大自然と向き合うフラの根本に敬意を払い、日本人として異文化の継承に真摯に取り組んでいる。

フラダンスのすべての動きには意味があって、昔カメラや映像がない時代に、旅人が見た素晴らしい景色や感情などを、歌や踊りなどにして大切な人に捧げたという歴史があるくらい。
フラそのものが言葉であるところから、僕自身もいろんなインスピレーションをもらっています。
知り合いを通じて新さんの踊りを見た時に、「日本人の男性でこんなに伝わるダンスをやられた人を初めて見た！」と感動しました。
それから、NHK Eテレの「Eダンスアカデミー」に出演してもらったり、自分たちの楽曲のフラアレンジの振り付けをお願いしたりしながら、ダンス語を作るメンバーにも加わっていただきました。

ÜSA's DREAM NOTE　239

FRIENDS

FATIMATA (Fatimata)

Fatimata is a pioneer of West African dance in Japan, bringing aspects of the traditional Senegalese 'sabar' dance and 'azonto' dance from Ghana.
In 2008 he coordinated EXILE ÜSA's visit to Senegal, and in 2010 choreographed the sabar dance for Gekidan EXILE's DANCE EARTH performance. In 2012 he appeared on NHK's E-Dance Academy as a translator for the Senegalese Wolof language. In 2016 he appeared on the same program to teach the azonto dance and introduce food and fashion from Ghana. He also supervised the 'today's azonto' corner of the program. He choreographed the track 'AZONTO' that appeared on the DANCE EARTH PARTY first album, produced by ÜSA in 2017. He performed 'AZONTO' at the DANCE EARTH FESTIVAL 2017. In 2019 he currently supervises choreography for the 'a-i-u-e-o dance' corner of E-Dance Academy TV program.
He holds dance performances, talk shows and workshops at international events and festivals, introducing the cheerful and colorful African culture, and selling clothes and crafts made from colorful west African fabric to share the elegant culture of Africa.

The azonto dance that FATIMATA specializes in is derived from everyday happenings, allowing communication with everyone.
FATIMATA's dance background and communication skills made him an easy pick to join the Dance Language team.

Shin Tanaka

President of Hula class Halau Keolakulanakila
Shin Tanaka is the only Japanese hula instructor endorsed by Hawai'ian national treasure George Na'ope.
After majoring in international relations at Eckerd College in Florida, Shin continued to a postgraduate course in cultural anthropology at the University of Hawai'i at Manoa. After researching the cultures of Hawai'i and Japan, he returned to Japan and began to learn hula in earnest from the late George Na'ope. Since 2003 he continues to practice hula under George Na'ope's trusted disciple, Kumu Hula Etua Lopes.
From 2002 to 2013 he worked as an instructor at his mother's hula school, taking part in competitions around Japan and abroad. In 2013, he became the first Japanese to perform as a Ho'opa'a drummer for Etua Lopes' Halau Na Pua U'I O Hawai'i at hula's most prestigious stage, the 50th Merrie Monarch festival. That same year he branched off from his mother's hula school, establishing his own school in Azabujuban, Tokyo, aiming to bring 'more smiles and color' to daily life through hula. In 2018 his school had its inaugural recital. In 2019 his class is the only one in Japan with over 50 male dancers. The hula Shin teaches is not so much a dance as it is an expression of nature through your body. Paying homage to the fundamentals of hula, a dance that reflects nature, he feels pride and sincerity as a Japanese person passing on the culture of another land.

In hula, every action has a meaning. Before cameras and movies, travelers used the hula as a way to tell their loved ones of the beautiful places and emotions they had experienced on their journeys.
The fact that hula is a language has been a big inspiration for me personally.
When I found out about Shin through a friend, and saw his hula for the first time, I was taken aback that a Japanese man could express so much through dance.
He has since appeared on NHK's E-Dance Academy, arranging our songs with hula actions, and joining the team to create a dance language.

AMIGOS

FATIMATA

Una pionera que introdujo en Japón el atractivo del baile "sabar" tradicional de Senegal así como el baile "azonto" tradicional de Ghana. En el 2008 realizó la coordinación del viaje de ÜSA de EXILE a Senegal y en el 2010 estuvo a cargo de la coreografía del baile Sabar del grupo de teatro EXILE en la presentación "Dance Earth". En el 2012 fue intérprete del idioma étnico wolof de Senegal en el programa "E Dance Academy" de E TV (TV educacional) de la NHK (emisora pública de Japón). En el 2016 participó en el mismo programa como instructora del baile azonto, además de introducir la cocina y la moda de Ghana. Además fue supervisora de la sección "azonto de hoy" que se volvió regular en el mismo programa. En el 2017 estuvo a cargo de la coreografía de "AZONTO" incluida en el primer álbum del grupo "DANCE EARTH PARTY" producido por ÜSA. En octubre del mismo año fue presentado "AZONTO" en el "DANCE EARTH FESTIVAL 2017". A partir del 2019 supervisa la sección "AIUEO Dance" que se ha vuelto regular en el programa "E Dance Academy". Actualmente también realiza presentaciones de baile, conferencias y talleres en eventos de intercambio internacional y festivales donde transmite la cultura alegre y colorida de África, además de dedicarse a la venta de accesorios y ropa de África occidental como parte de su difusión activa de la cultura y la moda africanas.

El baile "Azonto" de Ghana, del que FATIMATA es un experta, es un baile que consiste en expresar lo que sucede en la vida cotidiana para comunicarse mutuamente entre todos. Por ello, ¡FATIMATA es idónea para pensar en conjunto el idioma de baile! Es por ello que le hemos pedido que se una al grupo.

Shin Tanaka

Director de la escuela de baile hula Hālau Keolakūlanakila.
Es el único instructor de hula japonés aprobado por un hawaiano reconocido como tesoro viviente de Hawái. Estudió relaciones internacionales en la universidad Eckerd College (Florida, EEUU) y posgrado en antropología en la Universidad de Hawái en Manoa. Estudió las culturas de Hawái y Japón, y tras regresar a Japón aprendió hula de forma profesional del difunto George Na'ope. Del 2003 hasta el presente año 2019 es alumno de Etua Lopes, que fue el brazo derecho de Na'ope cuando aún vivía. En Japón fue instructor de Hula durante 11 años (del 2002 al 2013) en la escuela de hula de su madre, participando activamente en competencias dentro y fuera del país. En el 2013 participó en la 50a edición del Merrie Monarch Festival, la competencia más prestigiosa de Hula, como el primer japonés Ho'opa'a (percusionista) en el grupo Hālau Nā Pua 'Ui O Hawai'i dirigido por Etua Lopes. El mismo año se independiza de la escuela de su madre para fundar su propia escuela con sede en Azabu-Juban, aspirando a "una vida cotidiana con mayores sonrisas y colorido" a través del hula. En 2018 se celebra la primera presentación de su escuela. En el presente año 2019 se ha convertido en una de las mejores escuelas de hula en Japón, con más de 50 alumnos masculinos. Aparentemente, su coreografía busca expresar la naturaleza en sí por encima de "bailar". Cómo japonés se dedica con esmero a transmitir la cultura de otro país mostrando respeto a la raíz del hula, que es poner atención a la gran naturaleza.

Todos los movimientos del hula tienen un significado, y su historia consiste en transmitir a través de la música y el baile los hermosos paisajes y las emociones que experimentaron los viajeros en una época en que no había cámaras ni videos. El hula en sí es un lenguaje, y ha sido para mí fuente de inspiración. Cuando tuve la oportunidad de ver el baile de Shin a través de un conocido, me conmovió y pensé "¡Es la primera vez que veo a un hombre japonés que baila un baile tan expresivo!". Desde entonces, Shin nos ha ayudado presentándose en el programa "E Dance Academy" de E TV (TV educacional), con la coreografía de hula de nuestras canciones y también se ha adherido como miembro para crear el idioma del baile.

PROJECT ③

ネオテキーラ

NEO TEQUILA

大和魂×メキシコの太陽
和洋折衷の新しいテキーラを。

Japanese spirit x Mexican Sun
A new mixed-culture tequila

Espíritu japonés multiplicado por el sol de México
Por un nuevo tequila mezcla de Japón y occidente

NEO TEQUILA

僕の体験上、ダンスに一番マッチする酒。
それは、テキーラ！
ご存じの方も多いと想いますが、テキーラという酒は、メキシコ原産の植物であるアガベを原料に造られています。
このテキーラに、日本人の魂を込めて、
最強のお酒を造ってみよう、というのが、このプロジェクトです。

From my experience, the drink that goes best with dancing is… tequila!
Tequila is a Mexican spirit made from the blue agave plant.
This project sets out to make premium tequila that contains the spirit of Japan.

Según mi experiencia, la bebida alcohólica que mejor combina con el baile es: ¡El Tequila! Seguramente muchos lo saben, pero el tequila se elabora a partir del Agave, que es una planta de origen mexicano. Este proyecto consiste en introducir espíritu japonés al tequila para intentar hacer una bebida alcohólica infalible.

2012〜2018年にかけて6年間、本場メキシコのテキーラ村に通い、現地の蒸留所の人々と交流を重ねながら、僕の好みで、オリジナルのテキーラを製造しました。
その名も、「ハッピーラ (HAPPiLA)」。
飲めば飲むほど、踊れば踊るほど、ハッピーになれるテキーラが出来たと想います。

For six years from 2012 to 2018 I went back and forth to the town of Tequila in Mexico, the birthplace of tequila. While mingling with locals at different distilleries, I set about making an original tequila, tailor made to my taste. The name of this new tequila is HAPPiLA.
With HAPPiLA, the more you drink, the more you dance, and the happier you get.

Durante 6 años entre el 2012 y el 2018, estuve visitando el pueblo de tequila para tener varios intercambios con los destiladores locales, y produje un tequila original a mi gusto.
Su nombre es "HAPPiLA".
Creo que hemos creado un tequila que te hace más feliz entre más lo tomes y bailes.

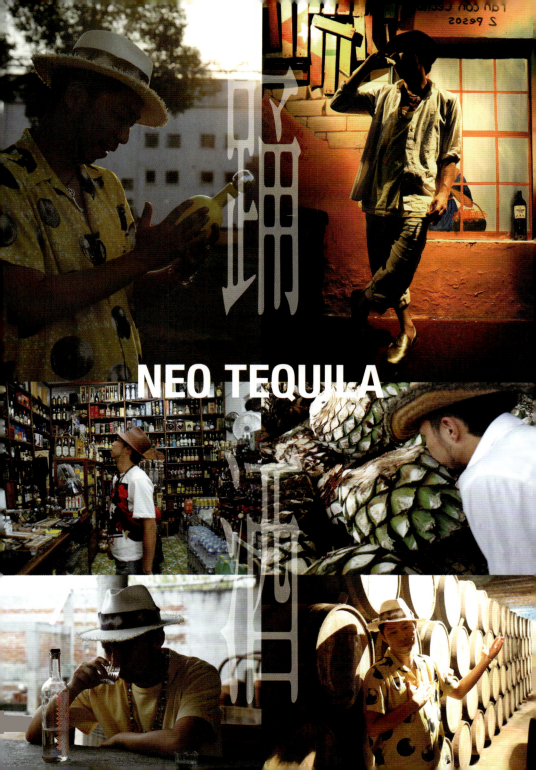

"HAPPiLA"がハッピーである**7**つの理由

ダンスや音楽をイメージしてデザインされた
オリジナル"ミラーボールキャップ"と白を基調としたボトルに
"レインボーアガベ"をモチーフにしたハッピーなデザイン

ブランコにレポサドを20％加えることにより
華やかでアフター・ノートにチェリーを感じるハッピーな味わい

"HAPPiLA"のアガベ畑は、火山や湖、古代遺跡に囲まれ爽やかな
風で木々のささやきが聞こえる、地球のパワーが溢れる場所で栽培

"HAPPiLA"のアガベは音楽を聴かせて育てているので
飲めばココロもオドル

100％アガベの"プレミアムテキーラ"なので
ナチュラルな風味が楽しめる

クリアな味わいなので、メキシコ料理だけでなく、
和食など様々な料理に合う

"HAPPiLA"という合言葉で乾杯すれば
世界中の人たちと仲良くなれる

そんな7つの想いが詰まっています。

Seven reasons HAPPiLA makes you happy

1 The happy bottle design features a mirror-ball inspired cap and white bottle adorned with a colorful 'rainbow agave'.

2 The happy flavor created by mixing blanco with 20% reposado is fruity with an afternote of cherry.

3 The fields where agave for HAPPiLA is grown are surrounded by volcanoes, lakes and ancient ruins, a place caressed by gentle winds and brimming with the earth's energy.

4 The agave plants used for HAPPiLA have music played for them when growing, adding a special musical spice. Drinking HAPPiLA makes your soul want to dance.

5 This premium 100% agave tequila has no artificial flavors.

6 The crisp, clear flavor complements not only Mexican food, but Japanese *washoku* too.

7 If you toast to HAPPiLA, you can become friends with anyone around the world.

These seven points make happy tequila.

---

7 razones por las que "HAPPiLA" te hace feliz.

1 Su "tapa de bola de espejos", un diseño original inspirado en el baile y la música, así como un diseño feliz de la botella con un ,"agave arcoiris" sobre un fondo blanco.

2 Un sabor feliz que deja un sensación de cereza, a través de una mezcla de tequila blanco con un 20% de reposado.

3 El agave de "HAPPiLA" se produce en un sembradío en el que prolifera la energía de la tierra, rodeado de volcanes, lagos y ruinas ancestrales y dónde se escucha el sonido de los árboles sacudidos por el viento.

4 El agave de "HAPPiLA" crece escuchando música, por lo que al tomarlo también baila el corazón.

5 Es un tequila premium hecho 100% de agave, por lo que se puede apreciar su sabor natural.

6 Tiene un sabor claro que no sólo combina con la comida mexicana sino también con la japonesa y otras cocinas del mundo.

7 Al brindar con la palabra clave "HAPPiLA", puedes hacer amigos en todo el mundo.

Éstas son las 7 intenciones que contiene el tequila.

EXILE ÜSA オリジナルテキーラ
EXILE ÜSA original tequila
Tequila original de ÜSA de EXILE
「HAPPiLA」
https://www.happila.jp

まだまだ、お酒プロジェクトも、始まったばかり。
これをスタートに、メキシコはもちろん、世界中の国々とコラボしながら、一緒においしい酒を造り、飲み、踊りながら、お互いを理解し合うためのハッピーなきっかけを、どんどん生み出していきたいな、と想っています。

The HAPPiLA tequila project has just got started.
From here I want to expand to other countries, collaborating with more people around the world to create more delicious alcohol, drink it, dance, communicate and create more and more happiness.

Aún así, el proyecto de sake acaba de comenzar.
Comenzando con esto, mientras colaboro con países del mundo, así como con México, creo que quiero crear más oportunidades felices de entendernos mientras hacemos, bebemos, bailamos y bailamos juntos. .

FRIENDS

林生馬

テキーラの奥深さ、楽しさを教えてもらった最初の人、それが日本テキーラ協会の林会長。

1968年東京生まれ。カリフォルニア州立大学で映画を学び、20世紀フォックス社にて映画制作スタッフとして活躍。ショーン・コネリーや北野武監督らとテキーラを酌み交わす経験を得て、テキーラの最先端の飲み方およびテキーラブームの到来を目の当たりにする。訪れたテキーラ蒸留所は100以上。
蒸留所のスタッフやテキーラ・アンバサダーとの親交も深く、日本へ帰国後の2008年7月に「日本テキーラ協会」を創立。テキーラ・マエストロ講座を全国で行う。
日本メスカル協会顧問。著書に日本初のテキーラ専門書「テキーラ大鑑（廣済堂出版）」がある。

日本テキーラ協会会長であり、日本メスカル協会顧問であり、東京ウイスキー ＆スピリッツコンペティション実行委員であり、ブリュッセル国際酒類コンクール審査員であり…… それでいて、遊び心満載のとても素敵な方！ メキシコで体験した、テキーラ飲み放題の車内で音楽や料理を楽しめる「テキーラエクスプレス」に感動して、福島で日本初のテキーラエクスプレスを実現させたとき、一緒にやっていただいたのも林会長でした。これからも一緒に楽しいイベントを作りたいと思える方です。

川上"カルロス"義貴

HAPPiLAを一緒に開発したメンバー、カルロスさん！
日本人だけれど半分メキシコ人のような……
仕事からプライベートまで、かなりのお酒を酌み交わしたアミーゴ。誰もやったことがない新しいことや、楽しいことをやっていて追求心がある。夢に向かって突き進むカルロスさんの姿に、共鳴しています。
そんな、テキーラの兄貴的存在、カルロスさんから頂いた素敵なプロフィールは、以下のような感じ！

「天真爛漫、自然に素直に育て」との家訓 (?!) のもと、底抜けに明るく過ごした少年時代。この家訓、天真爛漫さを原動力に、1ドル＝240円の頃、何もツテなく極貧渡米。カリフォルニアのサンタバーバラの大学に入り、「遊び、遊び、遊び、勉強」のローテーションでどうにか大学を卒業。その直後、日本の友人からメキシコの有名シンガーとの結婚式に呼ばれ初メキシコ。お城を貸し切って昼から翌日の昼まで騒ぎ踊り続けたウエディングパーティーでメキシコの熱さに見事にハマる。ついでにマヤ文明など遺跡にも軽くハマってしまい、とうとうペルーにまで。インカ帝国、マチュピチュ遺跡を見て、「なんて人間ってちっぽけなんだろう」と体感し、"カルロス"に変身。26歳に紫外線で色が発色するという素材、サニーカラーの海外販売代理店として独立。その後、衣料・靴の輸入などの貿易業を中心に運営。そして日本で初めてバンジー・トランポリン(www.scjinc.com)というキッズ向け遊具をイギリスの会社と提携して、子供向けのイベント事業も開始。世界中から"日本初""楽しいもの""かっこいいもの"を日本に紹介。その後、メキシコのテキーラの良さを強く感じ、日本にその素晴らしさを知ってもらうためテキーラ専門店通販情報サイト「テキーラムーチョ」(www.wazawaza.jp)をスタート！ また、2012年、新橋にテキーラBAR、2015年にはタコスBarもオープン。2017年には、海外に初進出。カンボジア、アンコールワット近くにブティックホテルをオープンし、2019年、その敷地内で、タコスBarとBBQ Grill restaurant barもオープン。

EXILE ÜSAプロデュースのオリジナルテキーラ「HAPPiLA」では輸入、監修を務める。

ラテンの熱いノリに、侍の義理・人情・大和魂を持った男を目指し、日々精進。
これからも From the world, To the world な男を目指しますっ！

FRIENDS

IKUMA HAYASHI

Ikuma Hayashi, president of the Japan Tequila Association, is the first person who taught me about the joy and complexity of tequila. Ikuma was born in Tokyo in 1968. After studying cinematography at California State University, he joined production company 20th Century Fox. Through drinking tequila with Sean Connery and Takeshi Kitano, he was introduced to the latest ways to enjoy tequila, and went on to witness the tequila boom firsthand. He has visited over 100 tequila distilleries, creating intimate friendships with distillery staff and tequila ambassadors. After returning to Japan he established the Japan Tequila Association in July, 2008. He conducts tequila maestro classes around Japan and is head of the Japan Mezcal Association. He is author of the only tequila encyclopedia in Japan, 'Tequila Taikan' from Kosaido Publishing.

Despite many faces and responsibilities as president of the Japan Tequila Association, head of the Japan Mezcal Association, committee member of the Tokyo Whiskey and Spirits Competition, judge of the Brussels Spirits Awards, and more, he still has time to create fun at any and every opportunity. After experiencing the Tequila Express in Mexico, with its free tequila, music and food, I set out to create the first Tequila Express in Japan with the help of Ikuma Hayashi. I look forward to creating more fun events with him in the future.

Yoshitaka 'Carlos' Kawakami

Carlos is co-creator of HAPPiLA. He's Japanese by blood but Mexican by nature. I've had more than a few drinks with this amigo over the years, both for work and pleasure. His curiosity leads him to try anything fun, especially if no one has ever done it before. I love watching him chasing his dream with all his heart. My big tequila brother sent me his profile below.

My youth was blazing bright thanks to my family's teaching; "as you are, true to nature." With this simple innocence, I set off to the USA when the dollar was still trading at 240yen, practically broke from the get-go. I entered Santa Barbara university, and through a cycle of play, play, play, study, I somehow managed to graduate. Soon after, I was invited to Mexico to attend my friend's wedding to a famous Mexican singer. We partied from noon until noon the next day at a rented castle, and I instantly fell in love with the Mexican spirit. I also got interested in ancient ruins and Mayan culture, and somehow ended up in Peru. Upon visiting Machu Pichu in the Inca Empire, I realized how insignificant humans are in the grand scale of things. At age 26 I set up an overseas sales agency for Sunny Color, a photochromic material that shows when exposed to UV light, and went on to trade in apparel and shoes. I later established a children's events company using the first bungee trampolines (www.scjinc.com) imported into Japan from the UK. I made a point of introducing 'firsts,' 'fun' and 'cool' things to Japan. Later I fell in love with Mexican tequila, and started a tequila specialty sales and information site Tequila Mucho (www.wazawaza.jp) to promote tequila in Japan. In 2012 I opened a tequila bar in Shimbashi (downtown Tokyo), then a taco bar in 2015. In 2017 I branched overseas, opening a boutique hotel near Angkor Wat in Cambodia, and adding a taco bar and barbecue grill restaurant bar in 2019.

I oversee importing of EXILE ÜSA's original tequila HAPPiLA. I spend each day working towards my goal of becoming Latino hot, with the spirit of a samurai and a Japanese heart. I'll always aim to be 'from the world, to the world'.

AMIGOS

IKUMA HAYASHI

Fue Hayashi, presidente de la Asociación Japonesa del Tequila, quien me enseñó la profundidad del tequila y la forma de disfrutarlo
Nacido en Tokio en 1986. Estudió cine en la Universidad del Estado de California y fue parte del grupo de producción de películas de 20 Century Fox. Tras haber tomado tequila junto con Sean Connery y el director Takeshi Kitano, fue testigo de la forma más avanzada de tomar tequila y de su próximo auge. Ha visitado más de 100 destiladores de tequila. Tras regresar a Japón en julio del 2008, funda la "Asociación del Tequila en Japón", teniendo una profunda amistad con los trabajadores de las destilerías y el embajador del tequila.Realiza seminarios para maestros del tequila en todo Japón. Es también asesor de la Asociación del Mezcal de Japón.
Entre los libros que ha publicado destaca la "Guía de Tequila para los japoneses (título en japonés: Tequila Taikan, de la editorial Kosaido)".
Se trata de una persona estupenda con un gran espíritu lúdico a pesar de ser el presidente de la Asociación Japonesa del Tequila, asesor de la Asociación Japonesa del Mezcal, miembro del Comité Ejecutivo de la Competencia de Whiskeys y espíritus de Tokio así como juez del Concurso internacional de bebidas alcohólicas de Bruselas.
También fue el presidente Hayashi quien me apoyó para materializar en Fukushima El primer "tequila express" en Japón, inspirado en el "tequila express" que tuve la oportunidad de experimentar en México, un vagón con barra libre de tequila, música y comida.
Es una persona con la que me gustaría poder crear otros eventos divertidos en conjunto.

"Carlos" Yoshitaka Kawakami

Carlos, ¡Fue uno de los miembros con quien desarrollamos en conjunto HAPPiLA! Aunque es japonés, parecería mitad mexicano… Es un amigo con quien he compartido muchos tragos, como trabajo y en privado. Tiene un espíritu de búsqueda, de realizar cosas que nadie ha hecho o cosas divertidas. Ha resonado en mí la forma de ser de Carlos, que avanza con ímpetu rumbo a sus sueños. Este es el perfil propio que me ha enviado Carlos, quien sería como mi hermano mayor en el tequila.
Viví mi infancia con infinita alegría, bajo la enseñanza familiar (?) de "vivir con inocencia y honestidad ante la naturaleza" Bajo esta enseñanza y con mi inocencia como motor, viaje a EEUU en una situación paupérrima, cuando un dólar valía 240 yenes. Ingresé en la Universidad de Santa Bárbara en California, y de alguna manera me logré graduar a través del ciclo "divertirse, divertirse, divertirse, estudiar". Justo después de ello, viajé por primera vez a México invitado por un amigo japonés para asistir a la boda de un cantante mexicano famoso. Quedé cautivado por la pasión de México en aquella boda en que se alquiló un castillo para festejar bailando desde el mediodía hasta el mediodía siguiente. Al mismo tiempo me cautivaron las ruinas de la civilización maya y otras, por lo que también terminé viajando a Perú. Al observar las ruinas de Machu Pichu de la civilización Inca, me percaté de que "los humanos somos tan pequeños" y desde entonces me transformé en "Carlos". A los 26 años me independicé como distribuidor en el extranjero de materiales fotocrómicos que adquieren color con rayos ultravioleta, llamados Sunny Colors. Tras ello, administré mi empresa dedicándome principalmente a la importación de ropa y zapatos. También comencé negocios enfocados a los eventos para niños, asociándose con una empresa de juguetes británica para introducir por primera vez en Japón el bungee trampolín (www.scjinc.com). Se introdujeron " por primera vez en Japón", "productos divertidos" y "productos atractivos" de todo el mundo. Tras ello, percibí con fuerza lo estupendo que es el tequila de México, por lo que comencé el sitio "Tequila mucho"(www.wazawaza.jp) para que en Japón se conozca lo maravilloso que es el tequila. Además, en el 2012 abrí un bar de tequila en Shimbashi, y en el 2015 abrí un bar de tacos. En el 2017 nos expandimos al extranjero por primera vez. Abrí un hotel boutique en Camboya cerca del Angkor Wat, y en el 2019 abrimos en el mismo sitio un bar de tacos y un restaurante-bar BBQ grill.
También estoy a cargo de la importación y supervisión del tequila original "HAPPiLA" producido por ÜSA de EXILE.
Mantengo un entrenamiento continuo aspirando a ser un hombre con una pasión y sentimiento latinos junto con un sentido de obligación (en japonés "giri") y compasión (en japonés "ninjo") del samurái así como el espíritu japonés (en japonés "yamato-damashii").

MY DREAM NOTE

今回の人生。
僕たちは、この時代、この国に生まれた。

日本人としての誇りを胸に、
和の国の持つ、ピースフルなビートを、
世界中に響かせよう。

21世紀。日本。
新しい風は、きっと、ここから生まれる。

In this life, we were born in this time, in this country.

With pride for our Japanese heritage,
we spread the peaceful beat from this country of harmony.

21st-century, Japan.
A new wind is starting to blow.

En la vida presente.
Nosotros nacimos en esta época, en este país.

Con el orgullo de ser japoneses, hagamos que resuene en todo el mundo
el ritmo de la paz del país de la armonía (nota: en japonés "wa" que al
mismo tiempo se refiere a "lo japonés")

Japón, siglo XXI.
Quizás sea desde aquí donde comiencen a soplar nuevos vientos.

踊る

Let's Dance!

EXILE ÜSA'S BOOKS

DANCE EARTH

BOOK&DVD
発行・発売：A-Works
ISBN978-4-902256-16-1

2008.10.10 Release
Publicado el 10 de octubre del 2008

旅と踊りを愛する男、EXILEのパフォーマー・ÜSAが、ひとりの旅人・宇佐美吉啓として、世界放浪の旅へ。原始時代から変わらない「踊り」という世界共通の言葉を通して、国境も宗教も言語も肌の色も超えて、人と人が、心と心が、繋がっていく旅＝ダンスアース。

キューバ・ハバナ／アメリカ・アリゾナ／セネガル・ダカール／ブラジル・サルヴァドール／タイ・サムイ、パンガン島／フランス・パリ／日本・まるちょん

EXILE ÜSA is famous for his part in the Japanese music and performance group EXILE. His love of travel and dancing lead him to travel the world under his real name Yoshihiro Usami.
Using dance, a common language that hasn't changed since prehistoric times, he danced the earth connecting with people and hearts regardless of country, religion, language or skin color

Havana, Cuba / Arizona, USA / Dakar, Senegal / Salvador, Brazil / Ko-Samui / Ko-Pha Ngan / Thailand / Paris, France / 'Maruchon' in Tokyo / Japan

---

ÚSA, miembro de EXILE que ama los viajes y el baile, se lanza a un viaje por el mundo como un viajero solitario, bajo su nombre propio Yoshihiro Usami.　DANCE EARTH: un viaje en que las personas y los corazones se unen superando las fronteras, religiones, el idioma y el color de la piel, través del "baile" que es un lenguaje común en el mundo que no ha cambiado desde la prehistoria,

La Habana, Cuba / Arizona, EE.UU. / Dakar, Senegal / Salvador, Brasil / Islas Samui y Phangan, Tailandia / París, Francia / Maruchon, Japónarís, Francia / Maruchon, Japón

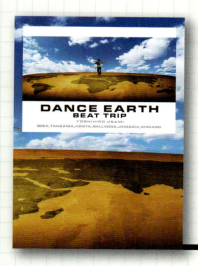

DANCE EARTH
-BEAT TRIP-

発行・発売：A-Works
ISBN978-4-902256-32-1

2010.10.11 Release
Publicado el 11 de octubre del 2010

踊ることは、生きること。生きることは、旅すること。踊ることが心底好きで、どんなときも踊り続けて、いつしか日本を代表するダンサーになった。EXILE ÜSAが、ひとりの旅人として、ビートを求めて世界をめぐる軌跡がここにある。

タンザニア（マサイ族）／ケニア（ギリヤマ族）／インドネシア・バリ島／インド／ジャマイカ／アメリカ・ニューヨーク／アメリカ・シカゴ

To dance is to live. To live is to travel. ÜSA's deep-set love of dancing has led him to become one of the leading dancers in Japan. But EXILE ÜSA is a traveler too. This is a record of his journey around the world, chasing the beat.

Tanzania (Maasai) / Kenya (Giryama) / Bali / India / Jamaica / New York / Chicago

---

Bailar es vivir. Vivir es viajar. A él le gusta bailar de corazón, y siempre continuó bailando en cualquier momento, hasta convertirse en uno de los bailarines que representa a Japón. Este libro contiene la trayectoria de ÜSA de EXILE, que recorre el mundo como un viajero solitario en busca del ritmo.

Tanzania (etnia Masai) / Kenia (etnia Giriama) / Bali, Indonesia / India / Jamaica / Nueva York, EE.UU. / Chicago, EE.UU.

ÜSA's DREAM NOTE 257

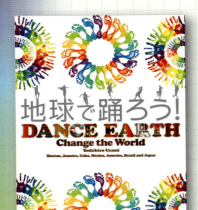

地球で踊ろう！
DANCE EARTH
-Change the World-

¡Bailemos en el mundo! DANCE EARTH
〜 Change the World 〜

BOOK&DVD
発行・発売：A-Works
ISBN978-4-902256-49-9

2013.4.10 Release
Publicado el 10 de abril de 2012

僕たちはダンスのある惑星(ホシ)に生きている。
EXILEのパフォーマー EXILE ÜSAの旅、第三弾。
「踊りで変える。踊りで繋がる。」をテーマに、世界中の人々と共に踊り、様々な人々と交流し、LOVE&PEACEを発信し続けるダンス・トリップ。

ブータン／カリブ（ジャマイカ＆キューバ＆メキシコ）／アメリカ ネバダ州 ブラックロック砂漠（バーニングマン）／ブラジル・ファベーラ／日本（福島＆ダンスアースヴィレッジ）

We live on a planet with dance. This is part three of EXILE performer EXILE ÜSA's travels.
This global dance trip is about dancing with people around the world, getting to know them and spreading love and peace with the motto, 'Evolve with dance. Connect with dance.'

Bhutan / Jamaica / Cuba / Mexico / Burning Man @ Black Rock Desert Nevada / Favelas in Brazil / Fukushima & Dance Earth Village Japan

Vivimos en un planeta donde existe el baile. Esta es la tercera entrega del viaje de ÜSA de EXILE.
Un viaje con el tema "Cambiar con el baile. Conectar a través del baile" en que ha bailado y tenido intercambios con gente de todo el mundo mientras continúa transmitiendo el mensaje de AMOR & PAZ.

Bután / El Caribe (Jamaica, Cuba y México) / Desierto Black Rock (Burning man), Nevada, EE. UU. / Favela en Brasil / Japón (Fukushima y Dance Earth Village)

日本で踊ろう!
DANCE EARTH JAPAN

¡Bailemos en Japón! DANCE EARTH JAPAN

発行・発売：A-Works
ISBN978-4-902256-58-1

2014.8.11 Release
Publicado el 11 de agosto de 2014

『僕らの国は踊る国！ ニッポンで踊ろう!!』日本人の心には八百万の神、すべてのものに神が宿るという素晴らしい教えがあり、その神々の数だけ、踊りや祭りがある。数えられるだけでも60万近くの祭りがあると言う。世界中のリズムを踊りこなしたEXILE ÜSAが、日本全国の「お祭り」を巡り、日本の心を繋ぐ旅へ出た。

神話の国（出雲）／北海へそ祭り（富良野）／青森ねぶた祭（青森）／よさこい祭り（高知）／鳴門市阿波おどり（鳴門）／阿波おどり（徳島）／郡上おどり（郡上八幡）／姫島盆踊り（姫島）／まりも祭り（阿寒湖）／神嘗祭（伊勢）／火振りかまくら（角館）／阿寒湖氷上フェスティバル（阿寒湖）

'Our country is a country of dance! Let's dance in Japan!' Japanese believe there are eight million gods; a god in everything in existence. I believe there are just as many dances and festivals in Japan too. There are close to 600,000 different festivals around the country, and that's just the ones that have been counted. After traveling the world and dancing to the world's rhythms, EXILE ÜSA returns to Japan to tour the country's festivals, connecting the hearts of Japan.

Shinwanokuni (Izumo) / Hokkaido Heso Matsuri (Furano) / Aomori Nebuta Matsuri (Aomori) / Yosakoi Matsuri (Kochi) / Naruto-shi Awaodori (Naruto) / Awaodori (Tokushima) / Gujo-odori (Gujo Hachiman) / Himeshima Bon-odori (Himeshima) / Marimo Matsuri (Lake Akan) / Kannamesai (Ise) / Hifuri Kamakura (Kakunodate) / Akanko Hyojo Festival (Lake Akan)

¡Nuestro país es un país que baila! ¡Bailemos en Japón! En el corazón de los japoneses se encuentra la enseñanza de que todas las cosas residen dioses, llamada "Yaoyorozu no Kami" (nota: literalmente "8 millones de dioses") y por cada uno de los dioses existe un festival "Matsuri" (nota: festival tradicional japonés). Se afirma que existen cerca de 600 mil festivales Matsuri según los que se han contado. Tras haber bailado los ritmos de todo el mundo, ÜSA de EXILE ha salido de viaje para recorrer los festivales Matsuri de todo Japón y conectarse con el corazón del país.

El país de la mitología (Izumo) / Hokkai Heso Matsuri (Furano) / Aomori Nebuta Matsuri (Aomori) / Yosakoi Matsuri (Kochi) / Narutoshi Awa Odori (Naruto) / Awa Odori (Tokushima) / Gujo Odori (Gujo-Hachiman) / Himeshima Bon-Odori (Himeshima) / Marimo Matsuri (Lago Akan) / Kannamesai (Ise) / Hiburikamakura (Kakunodate) / Festival de Hielo del Lago Akan (Lago Akan)

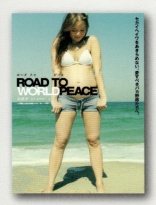

ROAD TO WORLD PEACE
著：高橋歩／監修：関根健次／協力：Next Wisdom Foundation

Author: Ayumu Takahashi
Supervisor: Kenji Sekine
Support: Next Wisdom Foundation

セカイヘイワをあきらめない、愛すべきバカ野郎たちへ。
To all the wonderful fools who won't give up on world peace.

2019.6 Released

僕らの一歩で、世界は変わる。まずは、世界を知ることから。
おもいっきり楽しみながら、自分なりの一歩を踏み出そう！

世界平和なんて言っても、難しいことはよくわからないけど・・・
もし、自分にも出来ることがあるなら、世界中の苦しんでいる人のために、何か役に立てたら嬉しいな。
そんな気持ちを持っているアナタへ贈る。世界中に溢れている「希望」を集めたアートブック。

Our actions can change the world. The first step is to learn about the world. Enjoy taking each step in your own, original way. World peace is a complicated issue, but there must be something we can do as individuals, to help the people suffering around the world in some way. If you agree, then this book is for you. This art book is a collection of 'hope' from around the world.

CHANGE THE WORLD
著：井上高志（株式会社LIFULL代表取締役）

Author: Takashi Inoue (CEO LIFULL Co., Ltd.)

誰もが幸せになれる世の中を、本気で創ろう。
Let's get serious about creating a world where everyone can be happy.

2019.Summer To be released

同じように、世界を変えようという人。
スイッチ切り替えて、本気で一緒に走るなら、僕も本気で応援するよ。

本気で世界平和を実現させようとしている経営者 株式会社LIFULL代表取締役社長・井上高志が贈る
世界を変えたい同志たちへの熱きメッセージ集！
誰もが参加できる現在進行中のプロジェクトも多数紹介！

More people are starting to think this way. If you're ready to get serious and go the hard yards, then I'm serious about supporting you. Takashi Inoue, CEO of LIFULL Co., Ltd. is serious about creating world peace. This collection of messages aimed at likeminded people is full of passion, and introduces current projects anyone can get involved in.

WORLD PEACE BOOKS

Official Website:
WORLD PEACE PROJECT http://wpp.blue

ALOHA LETTER

文：高橋歩／絵：DRAGON76／英訳：ロバート・ハリス

Text: Ayumu Takahashi
Art: DRAGON76
Translation: Robert Harris

2019.6 Released

もし、世界中の子どもたちが友達になったら…？

太平洋に浮かぶ美しい島から始まる、楽しい革命の物語。

What if you could make friends with children around the world?
This fun story of revolution begins on a beautiful island in the Pacific...

世界中の子どもたちが、みんな友達になって。互いに成長しながら、創りあげていく未来の地球。
それは、とっても明るく見える。国際協力や海外支援も大切だけど、もっとシンプルに、
「ダチが困ってるんだから、助けるのはあたりまえでしょ」って、
個人個人が自然に助けあうようになったら、素敵だよね。
そんなピースフルな世界を、本当に実現していくために。
ひとつの提案の意味も込めて、物語を描いてみたいな…
そんな気持ちが、この本の始まりだった。
世の中の大きなシステムを変えていくのは、
きっと、心の中でキラキラしている、小さなファンタジーなんだ。

**世界を魅了するアーティスト・DRAGON76×作家・高橋歩のコラボレーション絵本。
ついに登場！**

If the children of the world all became friends, and set out to create a future together, that would surely be a wonderful world. International cooperation and government aid are important too, but let's not forget the simple idea that it's human nature to help your friends when they are in need. Wouldn't it be great if we all did this as individuals? This book began as an idea; a vision of such a peaceful world that hopefully someday will become a reality. The power to change the massive systems of the world is in the small fantasies dancing in your heart.
A collaboration between globally renowned artist DRAGON76 and author Ayumu Takahashi.

著者プロフィール

高橋歩　Ayumu Takahashi

1972年東京生まれ。自由人。

20歳の時、映画「カクテル」に憧れ、大学を中退し、仲間とアメリカンバー「ROCKWELL'S」を開店。2年間で4店舗に広がる。

23歳の時、すべての店を仲間に譲り、プータローに。自伝を出すために、出版社「サンクチュアリ出版」を設立。自伝『毎日が冒険』をはじめ、数々のベストセラーを世に送り出す。

26歳の時、愛する彼女・さやかと結婚。出版社を仲間に譲り、すべての肩書きをリセットし、再びプータローに。結婚式3日後から、妻とふたりで世界一周の旅へ。約2年間で、南極から北極まで世界数十カ国を放浪の末、帰国。

2001年、沖縄へ移住。音楽と冒険とアートの溢れる自給自足のネイチャービレッジ「ビーチロックビレッジ」を創り上げる。同時に、作家活動を続けながら、東京、ニューヨークにて、自らの出版社を設立したり、東京、福島、ニューヨーク、バリ島、インド、ジャマイカで、レストランバー＆ゲストハウスを開店したり、インド、ジャマイカで、現地の貧しい子どもたちのためのフリースクールを開校するなど、世界中で、ジャンルにとらわれない活動を展開。

2008年、結婚10周年を記念し、家族4人でキャンピングカーに乗り、世界一周の旅に出発。2011年、東日本大震災を受けて、旅を一時中断。宮城県石巻市に入り、ボランティアビレッジを立ち上げ、2万人以上の人々を受け入れながら、復興支援活動を展開。現在も、石巻市・福島市を中心に、様々なプロジェクトを進行中。

2013年、約4年間に渡る家族での世界一周の旅を終え、ハワイ・ビッグアイランドへ拠点を移す。

現在、著作の累計部数は200万部を超え、英語圏諸国、韓国、台湾など、海外でも広く出版されている。

[official web site] http://www.ayumu.ch

EXILE ÜSA

2001年「EXILE」のPerformerとして、「Your eyes only 〜曖昧なぼくの輪郭〜」でデビュー。

2006年より「ダンスは世界共通言語」をテーマに個人プロジェクトDANCE EARTHの活動を開始し、世界各国の踊りを直に体感する旅に出る。これまでに20カ国以上のその土地由来のビートを乗りこなし、そこで得た経験を基に書籍、絵本、舞台、映像作品の制作など様々な形で自身の想いを発表している。2013年からは「DANCE EARTH JAPAN」と題し、日本全国の祭りに参加し日本を踊る旅を開始。2014年から毎年1月に東京ドームで開催されている「ふるさと祭り東京」の日本の祭りナビゲーターを務める。

2018年7月14、15、16日には幕張海浜公園Gブロックにて第3回目となる「DANCE EARTH FESTIVAL 2018」を3日間に拡大して開催。国内外様々なジャンルのアーティストがゲスト出演し子どもから大人まで楽しめるDANCE EARTHの世界観を表現。

NHK Eテレで2013年から放送されている「Eダンスアカデミー」では主任講師を務めている。

2018年5月からは国連WFPサポーターとして活動。飢餓ゼロに向けて発信。

同年6月産経新聞100歳時代プロジェクトアドバイザーに就任。

2019年2月2日オリジナルテキーラ「HAPPiLA」を発表。メキシコ大使館公認テキーラPR大使も務める。

[official web site] http://www.dance-earth.com

About the Authors

Ayumu Takahashi

Ayumu Takahashi is a modern-day Bohemian born in Tokyo in 1972. Inspired by the movie Cocktail, he quit university and set up American-style bar ROCKWELL'S with his friends at age 20, expanding a further three bars over the following two years. At age 23 he left management of the bars to his friends, and established Sanctuary Publishing in order to publish his autobiography Every Day is an Adventure, which became a bestseller along with numerous other literary works.

At 26 he married the love of his life, Sayaka, and left his publishing agency in the hands of friends to once again follow his dreams. Three days after their wedding, the couple set off on a global adventure taking them from Antarctica to the north pole and dozens of countries in between, before returning to Japan two years later. In 2001 he moved to Okinawa where he set up Beach Rock Village, a self-sufficient nature village brimming with music, adventure, and art. His projects around the globe span various genres and include establishing publishing companies in Tokyo and New York to publish his subsequent literary works, setting up restaurants, bars, and guest houses in such locations as Tokyo, Fukushima, New York, Bali, India, and Jamaica, and opening free schools for impoverished children in India and Jamaica. In 2008, to mark their 10th wedding anniversary, the family of four set off around the world in a camping car. After the mega-quake off Tohoku in 2011, he put the adventure on hold, returning to Japan to establish a volunteer village in Ishinomaki, Miyagi Prefecture, which has worked with over 20,000 volunteers and continues to support reconstruction of the region. He continues to manage a variety of projects in Ishinomaki and Fukushima. In 2013 the family settled down on the Big Island of Hawaii, bringing their four-year global adventure to a close. His literary works have sold over two million copies and have been published in Korea, Taiwan, and numerous English-speaking countries.

[official website] www.ayumu.ch

EXILE ÜSA

EXILE ÜSA debuted as a performer with Japanese boy-band EXILE with the hit single 'Your eyes only: Aimai na Boku no Katachi' in 2001. In 2006 he began his personal project DANCE EARTH, traveling the world experiencing the world's dances firsthand under the premise that 'dance is the world's common language'. He has taken his experiences dancing to the beats of over 20 countries to share his thoughts through books, picture books, live performances and videos. In 2013 he began participating in festivals around Japan, dancing his way around the country under the theme DANCE EARTH JAPAN. Since 2014 he has been the Japanese festival navigator at the annual Furusato Matsuri Tokyo held at Tokyo Dome every January. The third DANCE EARTH FESTIVAL at G-Block of Makuhari Kaihin Koen in July 2018 was extended to three days, featuring guest artists covering a wide range of genres, showcasing the DANCE EARTH world view for young and old alike. He is the lead instructor for popular TV program E-Dance Academy, shown on NHK E-TV since 2013. Since May 2018 he has been an official supporter of the UN WFP, promoting awareness for eliminating world hunger. He began his role as advisor for the Sankei Shimbun '100-sai Jidai Project' in June 2018. He announced his original brand tequila HAPPiLA on February 2, 2019, and is a tequila ambassador for the Mexican embassy in Japan.

[official web site] http://www.dance-earth.com

NE ZIPANG
ネオ ジ パ ン グ

2019年6月28日　初版発行

編著　高橋歩・EXILE ÜSA
Written and edited by Ayumu Takahashi & EXILE ÜSA

デザイン　高橋実／イラスト　ナナホシ
Design: Minoru Takahashi / Illustration: NANAHOSHI

翻訳　Ken Rhodes (英語)、グティエレス一郎 (スペイン語)
Translation: Ken Rhodes (English), Ichiro Gutierrez (Spanish)

編集　滝本洋平
Supervising editor: Yohei Takimoto

原案＆SPECIAL THANKS　磯尾克行
Original concept & special thanks: Katsuyuki Isoo

<協力> 株式会社LDH JAPAN、株式会社NTTドコモ、田舎館村企画観光課、行田市農政課、天明屋尚、エイベックス・エンタテインメント株式会社、ちかけん、竜馬四重奏、株式会社オフィスウォーカー、SHUHALLY、超歌舞伎、株式会社ドワンゴ、松竹株式会社、DRUM TAO、株式会社タオ・エンターテイメント、TOTO株式会社、JAXA(宇宙航空研究開発機構)、池下章裕、日本コカ・コーラ株式会社、株式会社バーソン・コーン＆ウルフ・ジャパン、株式会社ニチレイ、元祖食品サンプル屋 合羽橋店、株式会社岩崎、株式会社miura-ori lab、キリン株式会社、西田シャトナー、西山温泉 慶雲館、大江戸温泉物語ホテルズ＆リゾーツ株式会社、春花園BONSAI美術館、The Joinery (@TheJoinery_jp)、株式会社集英社、バードスタジオ、世界コスプレサミット(WCS)、カプセル・イン大阪、ニュージャパン観光株式会社、The Millennials、株式会社グローバルエージェンツ、9h(ナインアワーズ)、hotel zen tokyo、株式会社山本寛斎事務所、FEMM、SUPER TWINS、株式会社アークプロダクション、レスリー・キー、株式会社シグノ

<写真提供> ©getty images / ©アフロ / ©iStockphoto.com/ dikobraziy, Nirad, fzant, JianGang Wang, wdeon, manjik, jepler, mizoula, kvap, yakushige, Mlenny, TommL, kazoka30, Nayomiee, kohei_hara, kazunoriokazaki, bluesky85, kyonntra, mrtom-uk, Wako Megumi, Aleksey_Panov, tdub303, BrendanHunter, keng114, AH86, wutwhanfoto, georgeclerk, franckreporter, RichLegg, iryouchin, Yue_, Koji_Ishii, RichLegg, kohei_hara, Yagi-Studio, JazzIRT, electravk, georgeclerk, Xacto, bee32, Kwanchai_Khammuean, FilippoBacci, zomby007, xavierarnau, SeanPavonePhoto, LeoPatrizi, Kommercialize, PpcCreativeStudio, JianGang Wang, aozora1, ahirao_photo, catchlights_sg, powerofforever, JKKIM, Paolo_Toffanin, Zheka-Boss, mura, magicflute002, gyro, ES3N, Lcc54613, Casanowe, SeanPavonePhoto, coward_lion, Yulia Lisitsa, thanyarat07, ColobusYeti, Wenbin, winhorse, GOTO_TOKYO, mtreasure, kazushige hattori, Starcevic, brize99, coward_lion, 501room, matteusus, Cesare Ferrari, ksana-gribakina, atosan, minddream, JGalione, yaophotograph, SeanPavonePhoto, CHUNYIP WONG, Shi Zheng, baihoen, helovi, MarkMirror, nattya3714, imagenavi, Shoko Shimabukuro, vanbeets, ooyoo, Nikontiger, n_patana, Luckykot, Grafissimo, javarman3, Lusyaya, undefined undefined, Atiwat Studio, magicflute002, hichako, coward_lion, breath10, NaokiKim, voyata, Basya555, Coral222, pma2010, azuki25, 35007, Atypeek ©Adobe Stock mnimage, mtaira, 安ちゃん / stock.adobe.com ©PIXTA Fast&Slow, ahirun / PIXTA

印刷・製本　株式会社光邦

発行者　高橋歩

発行・発売　株式会社A-Works
〒113-0023 東京都文京区向丘 2-14-9 ／ URL：http://www.a-works.gr.jp/　E-MAIL：info@a-works.gr.jp

営業　株式会社サンクチュアリ・パブリッシング
〒113-0023 東京都文京区向丘 2-14-9 ／ TEL：03-5834-2507　FAX：03-5834-2508

本書の内容を無断で複写・複製・転載・データ配信することを禁じます。
乱丁、落丁本は送料小社負担にてお取り替えいたします。

©Ayumu Takahashi, EXILE ÜSA 2019

PRINTED IN JAPAN　乱丁、落丁本は送料小社負担にてお取り替えいたします。